Praise for
Broken We Kneel

"This is a timely project addressing the delicate and imprecise relations between piety and politics in contemporary America. It will help people in the pew discern a more active role in our national politics."

—Peter Gomes, author, *The Good Book*, and Plummer
Professor of Christian Morals and Pusey Minister
in the Memorial Church, Harvard Divinity School

"Diana Bass has written a moving, deeply personal, and provocative history of her struggle to be a peacemaker in the midst of post 9-11 patriotism. *Broken We Kneel* will resonate with everyone trying to live in the City of Man and the City of God."

—Bob Abernethy, executive editor,
Religion & Ethics News Weekly, PBS

"Whether through her down-to-earth stories about her daughter Emma, her insightful contrast of chapel and church or security and shalom, her reevaluations of Constantine and St. Francis, or her exploration of empire and its relation to the gospel of Jesus, Diana Butler Bass educates, inspires, corrects, and stimulates. I wish every Democrat in America would read this book, and then quickly pass it on to a Republican—including our President."

—Brian McLaren, pastor; author,
A New Kind of Christian; and fellow, emergentvillage.com

Other Books by Diana Butler Bass
Strength for the Journey:
A Pilgrimage of Faith in Community

Broken
We Kneel

Broken We Kneel

REFLECTIONS ON FAITH AND CITIZENSHIP

Diana Butler Bass

Foreword by Jim Wallis

JOSSEY-BASS
A Wiley Imprint
www.josseybass.com

Published by Jossey-Bass
A Wiley Imprint
989 Market Street, San Francisco, CA 94103-1741   www.josseybass.com

All biblical quotations are from The New Oxford Annotated Bible, New Revised Standard Edition, Third Edition.

Jossey-Bass books and products are available through most bookstores. To contact Jossey-Bass directly call our Customer Care Department within the U.S. at 800-956-7739, outside the U.S. at 317-572–3986, or fax 317–572-4002.

Jossey-Bass also publishes its books in a variety of electronic formats. Some content that appears in print may not be available in electronic books.

Library of Congress Cataloging-in-Publication Data
Bass, Diana Butler, date.
  Broken we kneel : reflections on faith and citizenship / Diana Butler Bass ; foreword by Jim Wallis.— 1st ed.
      p. cm.
Includes bibliographical references and index.
  ISBN 0-7879-7284-3 (alk. paper)
  1. Church and state—United States. 2. Iraq War, 2003—Religious aspects—Christianity. 3. September 11 Terrorist Attacks, 2001—Religious aspects—Christianity. I. Title.
  BR516.B365 2004
  261.7'0973—dc22

                                                          2003025356

Printed in the United States of America
FIRST EDITION
HB Printing   10 9 8 7 6 5 4 3 2 1

Contents

To the people of Trinity Episcopal Church,
Santa Barbara, California, especially
Mark Asman, Anne Howard, Ann Jaqua,
Nora Gallagher, and Clark and Terry Roof;
and in memory of two Santa Barbarans
who lived public theology,
the Rt. Rev. George Barrett
and the Hon. Walter H. Capps.

For we look "forward to the city
that has foundations,
whose architect and builder is God."
—*Heb. 11:10*

Foreword

After September 11, our nation in its shock and grief launched a "war on terrorism" marked by an attitude of holy war. It's been good against evil, us against them, and the slogan "United We Stand." But for many Christians, it has been a time when we deeply feel the tension between the demands of citizenship and the demands of faith.

American public religion, led by President George W. Bush, interprets our nation as good, pure, innocent, and morally upright—and our enemies as evil. The problem of evil is a classic one in Christian theology and in age-old Western philosophy. Clearly, the reality of evil in the world is real in the biblical worldview. Anybody who could not see the real face of evil in the terrorist attacks of September 11, 2001, is suffering from a bad case of relativism. To fail to speak of evil in the world today is to engage in bad theology. But to speak of "they" being evil and "we" being good, that evil is all out *there,* and that in the warfare between good and evil, others are either with us or against us is also bad theology. A simplistic "we are right and they are wrong" theology covers over the opportunity for self-reflection and correction. It also covers over the crimes America has committed, which lead to widespread global resentment against us.

Rather than taking a global view of God's world, it asserts the newest incarnation of American nationalism by confusing nation, church, and God. In effect, it places us above the Scripture's assessment of the human problem of sinfulness. It becomes a priestly civil religion rather than prophetic religion. A religion that invokes God's blessing on *our activities,* agendas, and purposes; rather than one that invokes the name of God and faith in order to hold us accountable to *God's intentions.*

Diana Butler Bass suggests that for Christians, a posture of repentance and humility before God, which she titles "Broken We Kneel," would be a more appropriate response. That prayerfully singing "Amazing Grace," is better than triumphantly singing "God Bless America."

She examines Scripture and history to come to a deeper understanding of "homeland," writing of our living in "holy insecurity" in God's city. Christians, she proposes, must consider every political issue theologically in light of the tradition, authority, practice, and wisdom of the faith community, with a keen sense of our primary status of "alien citizens." She correctly sees that Christians should always live uneasily with empire, which constantly threatens to become idolatrous and substitute secular purposes for God's.

The book ends with "an Easter epiphany," the realization that as we celebrate the resurrection of Jesus Christ, we are each empowered to be "a faithful alien citizen. To dream that the Christian story can make a difference in the world. To live a story of peace, reconciliation, love, and justice. To believe that there can be a place where people are free from oppression and fear. To give one's life to God's hope for humankind no matter the cost."

It is the word that being an alien citizen means living the resurrection and an Easter life; the word that, while we are in exile, we are to seek the shalom of the city where God has placed us and pray to the Lord on its behalf, for in its shalom we will find our shalom. *Broken We Kneel* provides us with thoughtful enlightenment as we continue to reflect on faith and citizenship.

Jim Wallis
Editor, *Sojourners*

Introduction:
"The Almighty Has
His Own Purposes"

While having dinner recently at a new Thai restaurant in Old Town Alexandria, my husband, Richard, and I began to cover predictable conversational ground: the war in Iraq, a story in the *Washington Post* about civil liberties and terrorism, the reassertion of civil religion and its effects on the presidential elections, and the book list for a course that I would be teaching in the fall on religion and politics. Faith, fundamentalism, terrorism, civil religion, violence, politics, and war. The restaurant's menu may have been new, but the topics for discussion seemed all too familiar.

Familiar? Inwardly, I sighed. Less than three years ago, few people could imagine such a conversation taking place on an ordinary night over Thai food. These things just were not on our minds. Yet now such conversations are taking place. Not only in suburban restaurants outside of Washington, D.C., but in congregations and church buildings, colleges and seminaries, in prayer groups and at Bible studies. Although it is sometimes hard to hear—perhaps due to the uncivil influence of talk radio—a lively, democratic discussion is taking shape in America's pulpits and pews, Sunday schools, classrooms, and coffeehouses. Americans are talking, and often arguing, about the role of religious faith in our national life.

Most people would not have expected these conversations. Few leaders, public intellectuals, ministers, or professors were prepared for them when they emerged. For nearly four decades, most observers and scholars thought the idea of civic faith—the belief in some transcendent dimension of American identity and destiny—untenable in the secular and pluralistic United States. Nearly three decades ago, in 1975, noted sociologist Robert Bellah published a book titled *The Broken Covenant* claiming, "Today the American civil religion is an empty and broken shell."[1] Despite resurgent fundamentalism and the growth of the religious right in recent years, the majority of cultural critics accepted Peter Berger's idea that the nation's "sacred canopy" of meaning had eroded and that American culture had, as scholars Wade Clark Roof and William McKinney said, "become too 'loosely bounded' to support a single and coherent civil religion."[2]

Whatever else happened on the morning of September 11, 2001, we proved that we were not loosely bounded. Indeed the power of our bonds—emotional, national, and communal—were demonstrated in thousands of ways and affirmed a sacred sense of our connectedness as Americans. Something transcendent gripped us. In the music of "Amazing Grace" and "God Bless America." In the unholy infernos of plane crashes and burning buildings. In the aftermath of fear and war. We know it is all about more than global capitalism and oil. There is something in all this about God and God's presence in our world, about being fully human, about grace and mercy, about good and evil. And despite all the attempts to find the "new normal," the more mystical—and mythical—bonds remain.

But to feel the reality of God through violent events, the agonies of terrorism and war and this new sense of human fragility does not mean we agree on *where God is* or *how God acts* in relation to the United States of America. In the autumn of 2001, it seemed pretty simple to most people: God was surely on our side; God defended and blessed America—and always had. In the intervening months and years, we still feel bonded by experience, but we are attempting to understand those cultural and emotional bonds in a more complex world than have earlier generations of Americans. We have discovered that we inherited our ancestors' civic faith. But that faith has been transformed by events of recent decades: expanded practices of human rights and individual liberties and increased sensitivity to religious and ethnic diversity and pluralism. We experience the bonds of civic faith in a vastly different world than did our grandparents. Our sense of nationhood, our civic piety cannot simply replicate the past. So we are talking. And arguing. About the meaning of faith, fundamentalism, terrorism, civil religion, violence, politics, and war.

When the media reports on civic piety, however, this does not seem like much of a conversation. Only one side of the discussion is being heard—typically the voices of those who believe that America is a Christian nation and who conflate God's will with American culture and politics. Just

3

yesterday, for instance, my husband heard a noted conservative author "exposing" the liberal attack on Christianity manifested by support for the separation of church and state and for prohibitions on such things as singing the national anthem in schools! Such manifestos, however intemperate, intolerant, or outright flawed, dominate the airwaves.

The other side of the discussion, the quieter side, is not taking place among radical secular humanists intent on destroying Christianity or any other religion. It is, rather, taking place among religious and spiritual people—Christians, Jews, Muslims, Hindus, and Buddhists—who are trying to come to terms with the American traditions of civic piety and the newer realities of religious pluralism. These Americans cherish the ideal of a nation "under God" but at the same time wonder exactly what that means in an age of violence, war, and terrorism.

I know about this discussion because I have been party to it. I am a Christian—a mainline Protestant one, a member of the Episcopal Church. I also happen to live in the suburbs of Washington, D.C., where I teach at an Episcopal seminary, and write about religious practice in contemporary America. For the last three years, I have witnessed something quite unexpected: neighbors, friends, students, colleagues, and fellow churchgoers all struggling to understand the relationship between faith and nation. For them—and for my family and me—that relationship has not been as simple to express as hanging up a flag or singing the national anthem at church. It has been difficult, divisive, and sometimes painful to try to reconcile the teachings of cherished Scriptures and faith community with the world of terrorism, war, and politics in which we live and work.

And it is tiring trying to be both a good Christian and good citizen. Richard and I have been trying to be faithful, to choose wisely, to work for peace, to follow Christ's teachings in this strange new world. As we talked at the Thai restaurant that night and finished up the last bites of basil chicken, we found our conversation was far from over. My husband asked if I wanted to go for a walk in Old Town.

"No," I replied, "I want to go and visit Mr. Lincoln."

"The Lincoln Memorial?" he asked.

"Yes. It's a beautiful night to go to the Lincoln Memorial. You know, it's my favorite place in the whole city."

We drove into the city and parked the car a short distance from the monument. In the midsummer heat, we silently walked past the Vietnam Memorial, a dark reminder of both that war and the one being waged in Iraq. A man dressed in full military uniform walked in front of us. We overheard him as he said to his companion, "I hope the president has been here recently." I hoped so too.

We walked up to the Lincoln Memorial and sat down on its cool marble steps. I looked around at the other people who had come to pay homage to Mr. Lincoln that night. Tourists and locals, blacks and whites, Latinos and Africans, Europeans and Asians, Christians and Muslims, Buddhists and Jews. Dozens of languages were being spoken on those stairs as people made their way to view the massive statue inside and have their pictures taken in front of one of America's greatest presidents. "Let's go in," Richard said.

I bypassed the crowd and went instead to my favorite place—the wall inscribed with Lincoln's second inaugural address. President Lincoln knew terrorism and war; he knew about good and evil. Yet at his painful moment in American history, he chose *not* to invoke God on behalf of victory for his cause. Rather, President Lincoln mused upon the complexities of faith and nationhood for both the Union and the Confederacy:

> Both read the same Bible, and pray to the same God; and each invokes His aid against the other. . . . The prayers of both could not be answered; that of neither has been answered fully. The Almighty has His own purposes. . . . With malice toward none; with charity for all; with firmness in the right, as God gives us to see the right, let us strive on to finish the work we are in; to bind up the nation's wounds . . . to do all which may achieve and cherish a just, and a lasting peace, among ourselves, and with all nations.

"The Almighty has His own purposes." Ever since I first read this speech, back in college, it has stayed in my mind. It is a powerful biblical meditation on the meaning of America, on suffering and hope, and on God's action in history. Of the speech's power, historian Ronald White writes, "We look back at Lincoln with ears that have come to anticipate a routine 'God bless America' as an expected benediction in the addresses of presidents and political candidates. Lincoln, on the other hand, was much less assured about God blessing America. He was continually striving to discern exactly how God was dealing, in both judgment and redemption, with the United States."[3] Mark Noll, also a historian of American religion, comments that "we have had precious few who, with Lincoln, have perceived how thoroughly the good and evil intermingle in our heritage."[4]

Perhaps that is why I visit Mr. Lincoln. To be reminded that seeing God's hand in human affairs is not simple—even when the world appears to be divided into good versus evil. God is the mysterious and sovereign One whose judgments, in the words of Scripture, "are true and righteous altogether" (Ps. 19:9). To live faithfully as a citizen in light of these transcendent realities is not easy. As theologian Reinhold Niebuhr would later say of the life of faithful citizenship, "It can proceed only from a 'broken spirit and a contrite heart.'"[5]

Over these long months, I have spent much time reflecting on the tensions between the demands of citizenship and the demands of faith. In doing so, I find myself in an ancient line of Christian thought. Since the beginning of the faith, Christianity's adherents have puzzled over the relationship between the new life that Jesus offered and the old ways of being that their inherited cultures established. The early church father Tertullian posed the question in the terms of biblical theology and classical philosophy by asking: "What has Jerusalem do to with Athens?" Tertullian's question is not only a philosophical one, however, it is also a political one—expressing the tensions between a way of life embodied in two very different cities. In recent months, I rephrased his question for contemporary Americans: What has Jerusalem to do with Washington? What has faith to do with the state? I confess: I have been tempted to respond, "Absolutely nothing."

But President Lincoln's words keep pulling me back— back to consider the "something" that does exist between faith and citizenship. I have come to some unexpected conclusions about church and state. Although many of my friends consider the idea of civil religion or national faith as spiritually or theologically vacuous, I do not necessarily agree. As a historian, I can say with some degree of confidence that recent events make it appear inevitable that the United States will always have some sort of civic piety, a public expression of its transcendent and theological dimensions. The question is not whether we will have civil religion; rather, the question is: What sort of civil religion will we have?

Since 2001, American politicians and American religious leaders have not done a very good job of either articulating the question or answering it. But the question of *what sort* of civil religion is the center point of the current discussions on faith and nationhood. And as citizens and as people of faith, we have some decisions to make.

The United States has different traditions of civil religion. Historian Martin Marty once grouped the two major traditions into the large categories of "priestly" and "prophetic" civic piety. Priestly civil religion tends to bless the established order that fuses a "historic faith" with "national sentiments." Prophetic civil religion, on the other hand, draws a distinction between traditional faith and the nation. But in its prophetic mode, civic faith holds the nation accountable to God's standards and judgments.[6] In a more recent book, Robert Jewett and John Shelton Lawrence further sharpened Marty's categories into two "contradictory" civil faiths: that of "zealous nationalism" (a militant form of priestly civic piety)

8

and "prophetic realism" (the tradition of viewing American culture as the intermixing of good and evil).[7]

The divide between priestly and prophetic is further complicated by an additional tension in contemporary American religion. For most of American history, civic piety was exclusive—that is, it interpreted God's actions in light of a single religious tradition: Protestantism. By the 1960s, the exclusivity of civil religion had broadened to include Roman Catholics and Jews. By the time this synthesis had been achieved, however, civil religion fell out of fashion. From then until September 2001, most Americans ignored or shunned civic piety. During those same forty years, of course, the country also became more obviously pluralistic. Thus, when civil religion reemerged as part of the nation's social fabric, the tradition faced a huge challenge: Upon whose God and what religion did it depend? Civic faith could no longer be exclusively Protestant—or exclusively Judeo-Christian. To represent who we have become, civic faith needs to be deeply ecumenical and represent the faiths of the whole world.

Will America's emerging civil religion be priestly or prophetic? Militant or realistic? Exclusive or ecumenical? These are the choices America's faith communities must make—and they are profoundly important because these choices will determine how we understand justice, peace-making, reconciliation, community, and America's sense of global vocation. In order to make the choices, however, we need to understand the questions.

What follows is not a political manifesto, not a scholarly treatise about church and state, and not an answer to vexing

9

religious questions. Rather, it is a theologically informed plea for prophetic realism in an ecumenical mode for American civil religion. As such, I confess that I am sad that American religious communities have not dealt very well with these issues in the last few years. Despite the discussions taking place, American churches have lacked clarity on the questions and issues at hand. This worries me as much as it saddens me. If religious communities fail to address issues of civic piety, then the practice of such piety is bound to be vacuous—a vague notion of God reduced to the lowest theological common denominator. In an age of religious diversity, people can be tempted to flatten faith traditions to fit current tastes and particular political agendas. In this scenario, the state can easily appropriate great religions for its own ends. The dynamism and robust nature of faith is lost, and tragically when the state uses religion, the mix often results in inquisitions, violence, and war. Religious people need to think long and hard about what binds us together as Americans and about the distinctive practices of our many faiths. Is it possible to express a public faith that both unifies and gives voice to our real diversity at the same time? Can believers hold the state accountable to the higher ethics and moral ends that our various faith traditions embody?

In addition to being sad and concerned, I also confess that I am angry that basically only one choice, that of zealous nationalism, is being offered in the public square. A conversation may be happening, mostly in places of worship, but part of it remains unheard, that quiet undertow of prophetic realism. I think Americans deserve the democratic process, as well as the spiritual practice, of forging a new sacred canopy of meaning together in community.

This book is, ultimately, a spiritual lament about faith and citizenship—a series of reflections on the events, experiences, and questions that sharpened for me the tensions between faith and nation. Because it is a lament, it is a personal book, one that springs from my own experience of Christian faith, informed by my vocation as a writer and teacher, lived in the context of being wife, mother, and churchgoer. This lament also testifies to my own struggle to be faithful, the struggles of some congregations in which I have worshiped, and the larger struggles of my own religious tradition, mainline Protestantism, to understand God and country in a world of religious pluralism, of terror and war. It testifies to that quiet conversation, the one happening in pews and living rooms, one so unnoticed that it sometimes seems only an internal struggle.

As a lament and witness, it is finally an invitation to journey with both one Christian and the Christian tradition into a conversation of faith and citizenship—one that has historical and contemporary dimensions. It is my hope that whether or not you, the reader, share my particular religious commitments, you may find an informative, reassuring, and yet challenging traveling companion along the way. And maybe some discussion fodder too.

With deep gratitude, I thank my friends, students, and colleagues at the Virginia Theological Seminary in Alexandria,

Virginia, for their support while I worked on this book. In particular, I acknowledge those who read the manuscript in part or full and who offered expertise and gracious suggestions for improvement: especially Tim Sedgwick, Jeff Hensley, Mark Dyer, Jennifer McKenzie, Will Scott, Sandra McCann, and Joseph and Megan Stewart-Sicking.

A few clergy friends also assisted in the process of thinking through the issues and revising the manuscript, including Randolph Charles, Church of the Epiphany in Washington, D.C.; Fritz Ritsch, Bethesda Presbyterian Church in Bethesda, Maryland; Bob Giannini, Christ Church Cathedral in Indianapolis; John Baker, St. Aiden's Episcopal Church in Alexandria, Virginia; and Tony Robinson, Plymouth Congregational Church in Seattle. Friends at the Alban Institute in Bethesda, Maryland, including Lisa Kinney Coburn, David Lott, and Claudia Greer, contributed to this project. Also, Br. Kevin Hackett, SSJE, carefully read an early draft and wisely counseled me on its contents. Other readers include my young friends, Jonathan and Leah Hartgrove-Wilson, whose commitment to living in imitation of Jesus Christ has taught me about the risks of discipleship. My friend Rebecca Adams remains an incisive critic. Any mistakes that remain in the book are mine alone.

Although they may not know it, this book began in the crucible of two phone conversations in September 2001—one with Craig Dykstra of Lilly Endowment Inc. and the other with Phyllis Tickle of *Publishers Weekly*. Each asked me probing questions about mainline Protestantism and the terrorist attacks. They may have forgotten these conversations, but I could not get them out of my mind. This book, although it may not represent their theological conclusions about church and state, is my response to their wisdom and insights about American religion and spirituality. I thank them both for their continued interest in and support of my work.

In the course of writing, I realized how deep an intellectual debt I continue to owe to my doctoral advisor, George Marsden (who has written extensively on religion and politics in America), and to the graduate program in religious studies and the divinity school at Duke University, where I studied in the late 1980s. Former classmates and professors, especially Gregory Jones, Jonathan Wilson, and Stanley Hauerwas, will certainly recognize in these pages that they were, indeed, right about some very important issues that I was unwilling to see at the time. Their influence can be found on nearly every page of this book, although the ways in which I interpret or express that influence is my own.

Many thanks go to Sheryl Fullerton and Jossey-Bass for believing in this project. Sheryl edited the work with her enthusiastic combination of friendship and professionalism—making it incredibly difficult for me to say no to the changes! Every author should be blessed with an editor who cares so much about a project, the book business, prose, and theological content. I thank her and her staff for all their help.

The dedication of this book to the people of Trinity Episcopal Church in Santa Barbara testifies to the power of God in community and to how that can continue to shape one's spiritual pilgrimage even after many years apart. Finally, my husband, Richard, read every word on every page—several times—and made me think hard about the issues herein. In many ways, he is even more passionate about this topic than I, and he was my primary companion on this journey. While I was finishing this book, my kindergarten-age daughter, Emma, learned both the Lord's Prayer and the Pledge of Allegiance—thus beginning a new generation of the conversation between faith and citizenship. To Richard, Emma, and my stepson, Jonah, my deepest thanks and love for your grace, wisdom, and compassion. The world is a better place because of your presence.

Alexandria, Virginia   Diana Butler Bass
February 2004

I

Broken We Kneel

ven though I am an Episcopalian and my tradition allows for it, I do not often confess my sins to a priest. I guess I am too much of a Protestant to feel comfortable with purple stoles and the spiritual intimacy of the confessional.

One morning in late fall 2001, however, my tender conscience got the best of me. In the upstairs hallway of Christ Church in Alexandria, Virginia, where I worked as director of faith formation, I told one of the priests on our large staff what I had done. I had taken the United We Stand sign— complete with the American flag—off the church's side entryway door. I was guilty.

"Yes, I did it. I just couldn't stand it anymore. I have to walk through that door every day," I told her. "I took it down."

I thought she would be proud. That she would agree with me and my furtive act of Christian rebellion. After all, I was standing up for the separation of church and state, for the clear witness of God's people as peacemakers, and for the church being in the world but not of it. Maybe if we had actually been in a confessional, she would have admitted to agreeing with me. As it turned out, however, she did not know I was seeking absolution for my trespasses. She was not expecting a confession.

"You can't do that," she said. "You can't do that." She worried, I think, about angering some congregants.

"I can't?" I asked. "Well, I did. I took it down. It doesn't speak for me. It doesn't speak for the whole church. I'm not united, and I'm not standing with the parishioners who put up that sign. Some people around here want revenge for September 11. I can't stand the thought of starting a war because of revenge."

"You can't do that. You work here. They put the sign up. It is their church."

Their church? *Their* church? Rarely have I been more stunned by something that an ordained person said. Since I was a little girl in Sunday school, my teachers and ministers had taught me one thing: the church is God's. We are God's. It is God's church.

"No, it is not," I replied angrily. "It is God's church. And if we don't speak for God around here, who will?"

Her pastoral side rallied as she gracefully asked: "This really matters to you, doesn't it?"

"Yes, it does. It matters more than anything else in the world. United We Stand is an excuse to commandeer the church for a military campaign against Afghanistan. I can't stand seeing all the flags hanging off the church. Hanging flags on churches feeds into the terrorists' hands. It mixes the

16

symbols of church and state and makes us religious nation-alists—almost like the Islamic fundamentalists. It is spiritual-ly and politically confusing. I'm angry and worried. I can't stand that sign."

"But it is their church," she insisted.

"No. It is God's church. If we keep those flags up," I threatened, "I'm going to put up my own signs. Alternative signs. Something about prayer, humility, and repentance."

I stopped for a moment, recalling an incident that had happened just a few days earlier at the grocery store. While loading groceries in my car, I noticed that the young man helping me was an Arab immigrant. I asked if he was alright, if anyone had been mean to him since the attacks. He did not answer immediately. Instead, he rolled up his shirt-sleeves. I saw bruises and Band-Aids from what looked like a recent trip to the Red Cross. He stretched out his arms, pointed to the marks and said, "I give my blood for the peo-ple of New York. My blood for New York." I stood shocked—in awe of the unanticipated theophany. He almost looked like Jesus! Submission to God, the humility of the cross, the blood of redemption, the unity of all people. No minister had ever preached the gospel better, and I felt my knees go weak.

That's it, I thought, as the vision pulled me back into the conversation. "I'm going to start the Broken We Kneel cam-paign. Not a flag. Flags are about victory. A cross. After all, that is what the New Testament teaches. Love our enemies. Pray for them. Pray for forgiveness of our own sins. Broken We Kneel."

My passionate rhetoric did not convince her. "You can't do that," she told me. "If you put up signs like that, it will start a war in the congregation."

Maybe this congregation needs a good argument over war, I thought as I went back to my office and closed the door. I reached into the box where I had hidden away the plastic stick-on United We Stand sign with the flag emblazoned above the words. I unfolded it and looked at the familiar stars and stripes. Sighing, I put it on my desk, turned my chair, and looked out the window. Broken We Kneel seemed a much more fitting slogan for Christian citizens—recognizing the limits of the earthly city, humbly bowing before God's wisdom, repenting of our lust for revenge, and forgiving our enemies.

On the windowsill sat an icon of St. Francis and St. Clare of Assisi. I thought of St. Francis's prayer, "Lord, make us servants of your peace; where there is hate, may we sow love; where there is hurt, may we forgive; where there is strife, may we make one." The healing blood of Jesus Christ, the mission of the church: peace, love, forgiveness, reconciliation. How hard it is to live as a Christian in a world that seems to be going exactly in the opposite direction.

I love my country—its ideals, its land, its history, and its people—but I love my God and my church more. My nation did not seem to be calling for peace, love, forgiveness, and reconciliation. It was mobilizing for war. Were we being forced to choose between the two? Was I the only Christian in America feeling tension between loyalty to my nation and loyalty to the reign of God?

That morning, I felt alone with St. Francis and St. Clare, alone in my worry and concern about the loyalty of the church amid terrorism and war and my growing sense that September 11 had opened a door for the church to be clear and powerful in preaching and praying for peace and reconciliation. I thought about the priest's comments: Whose church is it? Whom does it serve? And for whom does it speak?

CHURCH AND STATE AND TERRORISM

Ever since I can remember, two passions have framed my life—religion and politics. These twin passions have never sat easily with one another. There always seemed to be some tension, or some conflict, between my two interests. When I was a girl, my mother taught me that in polite company one should never discuss either.

But growing up in the Methodist Church in the 1960s, it was hard to avoid talk of religion and politics. Conflict between flag and cross created intense debates as we grappled with both the Civil Rights Movement and the Vietnam War. When I was very young, my church simply went along with both segregation and the war. By 1967 or so, new clergy pushed us to question these stances. Would Jesus treat black people the way Bull Connor treated them in Birmingham, Alabama? Was it right for soldiers to kill civilians in Southeast Asia? Was the United States always on God's side? Was God on the United States' side? The theological debates in mainline Protestant churches formed me in faith and citizenship.

Mainline denominations failed, however, to deal with these concerns in ways that made sense to American churchgoers. They vacillated between supporting the government and attacking it. Indeed, the lack of clarity around these issues drove many mainline Protestants away from church— raising questions about the role of religious belief in the public square. Does the Christian church bless the political order? Or does the church challenge it? Should Christians obey the government, or should the faithful protest injustice? In the 1960s, many churches never really answered these questions. They just waited for them to go away.

The relationship between church and state, between God's kingdom and the nations in which God's people live, is one of the oldest issues in the Christian tradition. For two thousand years, Christians have argued about the relationship between church and state, redefined it, and reinterpreted it. Entire denominations, like the Baptists, Mennonites, and Quakers, were founded on the theological belief in the separation of church and state. And social and political movements, including the American Revolution itself, were shaped by the ways in which Christians understood the spheres of government and faith.

Although the tradition is long and the questions were pointed during my childhood, they have slumbered uneasily for the past thirty years. September 11 changed that. The horror of the attacks, the threat to national security, the feeling of the world's hatred toward America all galvanized citizens, who started flying flags, trumpeting patriotic slogans, and pressuring their churches to support the decisions of our government in this perilous time. I had the uneasy feeling that Christians trusted the sword of the state more than the peace of Christ—or that they equated the two.

Despite my loneliness on that autumn morning as I stared at St. Francis and St. Clare, eventually I discovered a host of Christian brothers and sisters who were also troubled by the admixture of church and state that had arisen in American congregations. And contrary to the priest's concern that my Broken We Kneel campaign would split the congregation, I also discovered that nearly every clergyperson I knew—including her—was struggling during this time to preach God's good news of love, forgiveness, and reconciliation in meaningful, compassionate, and relevant ways to his or her congregation. But many of them, strangely enough, felt threatened by preaching peace.

Back in my office that day, I looked at St. Francis and St. Clare, and I asked them, "Why struggle? Why not simply wave the flag and sing 'God Bless America'?" After all, patriotism and the flag seemed to be helping millions of Americans summon courage. Why not enlist the church in the moral defense of the homeland? Why shouldn't I equate our cause with God's? I laid the United We Stand sign at St. Francis's feet.

I thought of some other words—words I had read long ago in graduate school—written by the Episcopal bishop of Ohio, Charles P. McIlvaine, to his congregations during the American Civil War, a time when political leaders almost completely appropriated the church for their own ends: "Let not the love of Country make your love to God . . . the less fervent. Immense as is this present earthly interest, it is only earthly. The infinitely greater interests of the soul and of the kingdom of God remain as paramount as ever."[1]

The kingdom of God. Where was that elusive kingdom of God? Certainly, part of the call of the church after September 11 was to serve grieving families, to give hope to the fearful, and to pray for peace, with its attendant values of liberty and freedom. But the Christian task was not to proclaim or even imply that our nation is blameless, morally pure, and divinely chosen. As witnessed to by nearly the whole Christian tradition, love of country is a lesser love than love of God's kingdom. American Christians are called to be servants of God's peace and, as the earliest believers of Jesus believed, to live as citizens of an *altera civitas,* another city, a better realm.[2]

THE CITY OF GOD AND THE CITY OF MAN

Christians often forget that they are citizens of two cities, which St. Augustine called "the City of God" and "the City of Man." The City of God has as its goal the love of God; the City of Man has as its goal self-love. The City of God recognizes its dependence on God, seeks wisdom, surrenders itself on a lifelong pilgrimage, and worships God. The City of Man, in contrast, believes itself to be all powerful, lusts for domination, covets money and possessions, and worships its own glory. The end of the City of God is a *telos* or consummation of communal joy with God and the saints; the end of the City of Man is destruction, its own death.

"In truth," writes St. Augustine, "these two cities are entangled together in this world, intermixed until the last judgment effects their separation."[3] Sometimes the City of Man honors the City of God and its virtues; other times, the City of Man will not. Depending upon the circumstances, Christians may live in harmony with the earthly city or in opposition to it. Or some of the time, we live with a realistic and limited sense of the earthly city's benefits. And some of the time, the faithful will be deluded by the earthly city, enticed by its deceptions, and enthralled by its power. But for those who follow Christ, the true home is God's city—always truer, purer, and more beautiful than any earthly one.

St. Augustine developed his theology of the two cities in the midst of the greatest crisis in Roman history. In 410 C.E., the barbarian Alaric and his Goths sacked Rome, the symbol of immortal civilization, the cradle of the Christian church. "Eternal city," bewailed St. Jerome, another ancient theologian, "if Rome can fall, what can be safe?" And as the monk Thomas Merton would write in an introduction to Augustine's book many centuries later, "The fall of the city that some had thought would stand forever demoralized what was left of the civilized world."[4]

Many Roman citizens fled across the Mediterranean Sea to the North African city of Hippo, where St. Augustine served as bishop. As a pastor, he looked out over his fearful congregation of refugees, men and women who had once lived at the center of power, in the most important city in the world, and he began to preach about war and peace, time and history, death and life.

The problem, Augustine proposed, was that Christians—comfortable with imperially sanctioned faith—had forgotten their true citizenship. Rome had been too alluring; Christians had confused its fortunes with God's blessing. When possible, Christians should avail themselves of the goodwill of the earthly city, but they must always remember that the earthly city and the heavenly city are fundamentally at odds. Each worships its own god—itself or the God of the Bible. The two cities may share some hopes and interests, but as St. Augustine states, "the two cities could not have common laws of religion. Here the heavenly city must dissent and become obnoxious to those who think differently."[5]

Augustine makes his case clear: no matter the glories of imperial Christianity, the Christian emperor and all his bishops, the state-supported clergy, the beautiful basilicas housing the celebration of the Mass, no human city can ever—in history past or yet to come—be equated with the heavenly one. "The heavenly city," he insists, "while it sojourns on earth, calls citizens out of all nations and gathers together a society of pilgrims of all languages . . . in its pilgrim state the heavenly city possesses peace by faith; and by this faith it lives."[6]

For the United States, September 11, 2001, was Alaric's sack of Rome. When the outsiders smashed into the centers of power, the unthinkable had happened. Many things went through my mind and heart as I watched the second plane hit the World Trade Center, but St. Jerome's words struck me once again: "Eternal city, if you can fall, what can be safe?" The peace of the earthly city of the United States had been destroyed; maybe it had been an illusion all along. And now, as St. Augustine's flock once had, American Christians faced the press of history, "like an olive press."[7] I wondered what oil would come from this harvest.

THE MARVELOUS PARADOX

Of Augustine on the collapse of civilizations, Yale church historian Rowan Greer writes in his book *Broken Lights and Mended Lives,* "The practical implication of Augustine's view is that what matters is to endure. The Christian can be neither fully involved in his society nor fully withdrawn from it. Instead, he must keep his sight on the pilgrim's path."[8] According to Greer, Augustine taught that life in the earthly city "must be taken seriously. . . . We must be citizens. Nevertheless, our experience is that of a pilgrim or a convalescent; it takes on its true meaning only when related to our destiny in the City of God. And so we are aliens."[9] During his press of history, Augustine concluded that Christians were *civitas peregrina,* meaning resident strangers or alien citizens. The ancient Epistle to Diogentus, an early Christian document not included in the Bible, refers to Jesus' followers as "strangers" and "sojourners" to whom "every foreign country is their homeland, and every homeland is a foreign country."[10] Greer calls this the "marvelous paradox" of being a Christian.[11]

Americans are not a paradoxical people. Practical and pragmatic, yes. Paradoxical, no. Because the state has been largely friendly to the church throughout American history, the state usually engenders Christian loyalty. Many Christians simply equate the goals of the state with the goals of the church without question. A few, more skeptical of the American government's historical record with the gospel, reject or challenge the demands of earthly citizenship. Thus, American churches tend to divide along these lines during times of crisis, for or against. As historian Mark Noll writes, "The dominant pattern of political involvement in America has always been one of direct, aggressive action. . . . Americans have moved in a straight line from personal belief to social reform, from private experience to political activity."[12] Obey the government. Protest its directives. Whichever one chooses, both assume "a straight line from personal belief to social reform."

But what if it is not a straight line? What if it is an olive press, the press of history, a turning wheel of chaos and suffering? What if it is a paradox, two seemingly contradictory ideas that are both completely true? What do "alien citizens" do when their society has been attacked, when their earthly peace has been disrupted, when the barbarians are at the gates? How does one live in a paradox?

Augustine's biographer, Peter Brown, says, "The members of the *civitas peregrina* . . . maintain their identity not by withdrawal, but by something far more difficult: by maintaining a firm and balanced perspective on the whole range of loves of which men are capable."[13] For St. Augustine, alien citizenship meant having a different vision than those around him—and being able to appropriately order one's loves according to the way of life taught by Jesus. It meant rejecting the earthly city's temptations of wealth and power in favor of the virtues of God's city embodied in the practices of hospitality, peacemaking, fidelity, hope, and charity. It meant being able to see past the earthly city to the parallel, sometimes difficult to discern, and alternate common-wealth.

Not everyone in the ancient world agreed with St. Augustine. And not everyone could see as he saw. Two cities? Alien citizenship? Even after its sack, many Christians wanted to rebuild the earthly city of Rome, to increase its political power, and to enlarge its reach around the Mediterranean world. Build the walls of the city thicker, higher, and safer—because it was God's will. Loving Rome was the same as loving God's city. Enforcing Christ's kingdom by might and law was the right thing to do.

But history proved that the quest to rebuild Christian Rome was a difficult one. In the centuries since, many earthly cities have come and gone, but Augustine's vision of God's realm has remained sure: "God himself, who is the Author of virtue, shall there be its reward. . . . He has promised himself. That city shall have no greater joy than the celebration of the grace of Christ, who redeemed us by his blood."[14] One may love an earthly city, but the love of God's city is the all-consuming vision of the *civitas peregrina,* living as God's people in this world.

A PILGRIMAGE OF VISION

I took down the United We Stand sign because it obscured my vision of that other city. And I believe it obscured the vision of the congregation I served. It revealed that the congregation had disordered loves. They either loved their country more than God's kingdom or they conflated the two. But it was hard see the "marvelous paradox" of alien citizenship because congregants drew a straight line from their experience to a political stance and action. Most wished for swift, aggressive action against their enemies. Rather than sojourners, they preferred to be soldiers. They believed the City of God and the City of Man to be coterminous, not commingled.

They failed to see something basic to a Christian way of life. Theologian Barry Harvey describes it like this: "There was from the beginning, however, one major difference between the pilgrim city of Christ and all others. This parallel *polis,* unlike every other city, had no walls, for it had no territory to defend."[15] The citizens of God's city may be found in every earthly city. They are scattered among the nations. Their unity in Christ transcends the divisions of ethnicity, class, and nationhood and constitutes a new people who embody God's reconciling peace. According to biblical witness, Christian citizenship is fundamentally at odds with violence on behalf of the state's political, economic, and geographical division of humanity.

During times of horror and chaos, congregations need to be challenged by the cross and see that it calls Christ's people to live as citizens of God's city. The flag may comfort them, making them cry and their hearts swell with pride, but its symbolic power—of territory, walls, and national defense—equally obscures the biblical story and Christian virtues according to which God's people are called to live. United We Stand symbolizes the earthly city's attempt to rebuild its walls and strengthen its fortresses.

From the perspective of classical Christian theology, United We Stand is full of hubris or arrogance, replacing the human city and its intentions with the love and justice of God's city. In the weeks following September 11, I found no comfort in the flag. Rather, every time I saw it fly, I remembered that I was a citizen of another city—one bound in the blood of Christ and the waters of baptism to millions of other alien citizens in all the world's nations, people striving to practice their faith in the face of violence, division, oppression, hatred, and poverty. That I was a sojourner, an alien citizen, an emissary of God's city.

This book is about one woman's quest to see more clearly; to try to sort out the strands of human existence in two cities; and to live for peace, love, forgiveness, and reconciliation. And as it happens, it is the journey of a witness who lived in Washington, D.C., when its peace was disturbed and those in authority desperately tried to restore a sense of earthly order.

For me, living in Washington has been a test of faith. Every day, amid terror threats, warmaking, and political division, I have to think about what it means to be a *civitas peregrina*. And daily, I have to choose a way of life that embodies the love of the City of God. It has not been easy.

In these pages, I testify to the marvelous paradox of alien citizenship. Fighter jets roar over my office as I write; I am learning to endure as a Christian. To live in the paradox. To be a Christian; to embody peace, love, and hope; and to live in this city and believe it can make a difference. To know that I am a citizen of a better city, one whose virtues and ends differ from those of my nation. To be an emissary of that other city. To look beyond the earthly city's travails to the peace of the city that is harder to see.

And as I have learned, sometimes the view is clearer from your knees.

2

"And a Little Child Shall Lead Them"

On the morning of September 12, 2001, I took my daughter, Emma, to her preschool—located only three miles from the Pentagon. No one knew what the day after would bring. Another attack? Go on, officials told us. Go on as normal.

But it was not normal. Wanting to shield her from the news, I switched the car radio off. We drove in silence, and she intuited that this day differed from others. While waiting at a stoplight, a little voice asked from the backseat of the station wagon, "Mommy, will this be another bad day?"

"I hope not, honey. I hope not. And if it is a bad day, Mommy will keep you safe. Just like yesterday."

Of all my worries following September 11, my greatest concern was for the children. My daughter. My stepson in California. My friends' children. The children—the living and the yet to be born—of those who died in New York and Washington. America's children. And the children in the far-off places like Afghanistan and Iraq who, I suspected, having known much fear in their lives, would shortly face the fear of American bombs.

As it turned out, I was not the only American parent worried about the children. Over the weeks to come, talk shows featured child development specialists advising parents on how to help their children understand violence and how to assure them amid their fears. Churches and denominations offered resources for helping children cope.

Many of these counselors suggested shielding children from the news, and thereby, I suspect, preserving some sort of romantic notion of childhood innocence and, in the process, stirring parental anxieties to support the government to keep their children safe. But as theologian Stanley Hauerwas has argued, "the having of children is not a matter of our being able to make sure the world into which children are born will be safe." Rather, he continues, "Children are the way we remember that it is God that matters, not making the world safe or rich."[1] For Christians, children are a gift of grace—not a possession to protect—through which both the parents and their offspring grow in the way of faith.

At the time of the attacks, Emma was nearly four, about the same age I had been when President Kennedy was assassinated. I remember few details of that week—that the grown-ups kept crying; that the *Baltimore Sun* was edged in a thick, black border; and that mournful music and church services replaced my cartoons on television. I did not really understand. Only that November 22, 1963, had been a bad day.

But those events, as incomprehensible as they were to a four-year-old girl, affected the course of my life—and the lives of my peers—for both good and ill. We would be formed by sorrow and disillusionment; distrust of authority;

an unpopular war; domestic turmoil; and powerful commitments to justice, human rights, and personal freedom for all. President Kennedy's death was the stage on which the 1960s and 1970s played out. That too had been a bad day. And more bad days would follow.

During the quiet drive on the morning of September 12, I wondered: *What would it be like for the four-year-olds of 2001?* They had been born to the prosperity and optimism of the late 1990s and plunged, without their permission, into a war without borders and without end. How would their story be shaped by these events? How would their faith be shaped by these things? And how could I, as a parent of such a child, help shape her to have a heart of Christian compassion and courage—so that she might faithfully live in a world remade on a bad September day?

In the weeks that followed, my daughter surprised and challenged me—responding to larger events in ways that taught me what it means to be both a trusting disciple and a Christian parent. She would help me remember that it is not safety but God that matters. As I relearned from her the lessons that I myself had taught her, I recalled Isaiah's vision for God's reign (11:6), an ancient promise that formed America's early spiritual imagination, and was visually expressed in the nineteenth-century painting of Edward Hicks, *The Peaceable Kingdom:*

The wolf shall live with the lamb,
The leopard shall lie down with the kid,
The calf and the lion and the fatling together,
And a little child shall lead them.

PURPOSEFUL PARENTING

I was in my late thirties when my daughter was born. I confess that my surprise rivaled that of the Scriptures' older mothers, especially the response of Hannah, mother of the prophet Samuel. Although I did not leave my infant at the temple, my heart resonated with Hannah's dedication of her son: "For this child I prayed; and the Lord has granted me the petition that I made to him. Therefore I have lent him to the Lord; as long as he lives, he is given to the Lord" (1 Sam. 1:27–28). My husband and I wanted to purposefully raise Emma in our faith and impart to her a way of life shaped by Christian practices.

Intentional childrearing is not easy. Too often, parents raise their children as if by accident—repeating patterns established by generations past. But for parents schooled in biblical tradition, childrearing is a process of formation, a faith practice itself, one that they must embrace with heart, be willing to act with risks, and conscientiously carry out. Biblical faith is a faith of generational intentionality: "Hear, O Israel: The Lord is our God, the Lord alone. You shall love the Lord your God with all your heart, and with all your soul, and with all your might. Keep these words that I am commanding you today in your heart. Recite them to your children and talk about them when you are at home and away, when you lie down and when you rise" (Deut. 6:4–7).

Even for the ancient Israelites, faith was not solely an ethnic inheritance. Faith, indeed, was a gift of God's love and mercy—cherished, taught, practiced, and passed on in and through community. Sometimes, as told in the narrative of the Hebrew Bible, the Jews forgot that faith needed to be intentional rather than assumed.

My parents assumed that their children would have faith—as they also assumed that we would join the Methodist Church and sit in the same Methodist pews as had *their* parents and grandparents. Good intentions aside, my parents did not recognize that, by the late 1960s, it had become impossible to assume Christian faith. The world had changed too much. Faith needed to be taught with joy, pursued with purpose, and given to the next generation. It could not be the stuff of once-a-week lessons in a chilly basement Sunday school.

Thus, for me, parenthood involved a practice of biblical storytelling to my daughter—where the world became, to paraphrase the Protestant reformer John Calvin in his *Institutes of the Christian Religion,* a living theology classroom and where all things are "ensigns and emblems" of God's grace.

HONORING OTHER FAITHS

One of my most challenging moments of such theological purposefulness came when my family moved to northern Virginia. My daughter, born in Memphis, was two. Back in Memphis, the world existed in three colors and two languages: people were black, brown, and white; they spoke English or Spanish. The triculturalism of the contemporary urban South was pretty easy for a toddler to comprehend.

In the cosmopolitan suburbs of Washington, D.C., however, multiculturalism exists at a level that even I found (and still find) challenging. Trips to the local grocery store and mall shocked and surprised Emma—as she heard unfamiliar languages and saw unfamiliar native costumes. Some of it intrigued her. But one thing frightened her: Muslim women wrapped in veils. Every time she saw a Muslim woman in traditional dress, she would point and say in a worried tone, "What's that, Mommy? What's that?"

One day in late summer 2000, after more than a few embarrassments, I turned the mall trip into a teaching moment. Emma saw a woman walking toward us covered in a veil and asked the inevitable, "What's that, Mommy?"

"Emma," I answered, "that lady is a Muslim from a faraway place. And she dresses like that—and covers her head with a veil—because she loves God. That is how her people show they love God."

My daughter considered these words. She stared at the woman who passed us. She pointed at the woman, then pointed at my hair, and further quizzed, "Mommy, do you love God?"

"Yes, honey," I laughed. "I do. You and I are Christians. Christian ladies show love for God by going to church, eating the bread and wine, serving the poor, and giving to those in need. We don't wear veils, but we do love God."

After this, Emma took every opportunity to point to Muslim women during our shopping trips and telling me, "Mommy, look, she loves God." One day, we were getting out of our car at our driveway at the same time as our Pakistani neighbors. Emma saw the mother, beautifully veiled, and, pointing at her, shouted, "Look, Mommy, she loves God!"

My neighbor was surprised. I told her what I had taught Emma about Muslim women loving God. While she held back tears, this near stranger hugged me, saying, "I wish that all Americans would teach their children so. The world would be better. The world would be better."

I had been intent for some time in teaching my young daughter to honor others' faith, to understand that Christians, Jews, and Muslims are all Abraham's children. Looking around the mall in northern Virginia, I knew that, as she grew, she would have to claim, cherish, and practice her own faith, and at the same time, she would have to honor—not just tolerate—the faiths of her neighbors. I did not want her to fear difference. I did not want her to demonize someone else's religion. She needed to understand that all people are created in God's image—and that God loves everybody—in order to be both a good Christian and a good American in this new century.

Only after September 11 did I realize that raising a child to honor the faith of others was a Christian practice with profound social and political consequences.

CHARITY

Not all lessons taught by intentionally Christian parents are quite as obvious, however. I am convinced that purposeful parenting is hard because mothers and fathers do not always realize how deeply they have been formed by their faith traditions. Some accidents of faithful parenting are happy ones.

However committed I was to teaching my daughter religious diversity, I took no special care to teach her about charity. Charity is one of those things Christians assume. By age four, she had sat through four church stewardship campaigns, given a weekly offering, and both heard about and witnessed ministry to the poor. We read stories of saints, sang songs, offered prayers of thanks, and taught her that all gifts come from God. Charity is just one of those things—one of the things Christians do, often without thinking—to show forth the love of God.

Once, someone asked me when I first remembered serving another person or giving money to the poor. I could not remember and still cannot. I grew up Methodist. As was the case with Methodism's founder, John Wesley, faithful Methodists cannot hang onto money. Church history records Wesley at eighty tramping through the snow emptying his pockets to the poor. Methodists just give money away. Besides singing, it is the most enduring Christian practice I maintain from my Methodist upbringing. Good Christians give to those who suffer need.

On the evening of September 13, President Bush called on the nation to go to church, synagogue, and mosque the next day at noon for special prayers. I worked in a church: with a presidential imprimatur, Friday September 14 was bound to be a big day. And an emotional one.

The morning of September 14 proved rushed. The family was late getting up—and my husband and I were preparing for a full, and uncertain, day. He was in the kitchen with coffee and newspaper; I was in the bedroom dressing.

Emma came into the bedroom. "Mommy, do you have any pennies?" she asked.

Pennies? "Yes, here are some pennies. While I get dressed, why don't you go and watch *Dragon Tales* on PBS?"

She did not go to the family room. Instead, I heard her in the kitchen. "Daddy," she asked, "do you have any pennies?"

Within a minute, she was back in the bedroom. "Mommy, can I have some more pennies?" Irritated, I gave her some more pennies.

Again, I heard her in the kitchen with her father. This time, when she arrived back in the bedroom, she was toting a plastic sandwich bag filled with pennies. She held out her bag and repeated her request, "Mommy, can I have some more pennies?"

What was this about? "Honey," I finally responded, "why do you want pennies?"

She looked right in my eyes. "I want to send them to all the killed people in New York so they will feel better."

I went down on my knees and hugged her. "I'm so proud of you, Emma," I said. "That's exactly right. When people are hurting, we help them by giving."

I do not know where she learned charity. But I suspect that, like her mother, she will never be able to remember the first time she gave to the poor or offered her hand to those who suffer. She did not collect pennies because she possesses some miraculous spiritual sense. Rather, she collected those pennies because charity is a virtue of biblical people. Both her parents and her church taught this and assumed it to be true.

A little more than a week later, I was sitting with a Ground Zero rescue worker on a train to New York. He worked with the Salvation Army, and he shared painful, wrenching stories about the experience.

I thanked him for his work. And as a gift, I told him about Emma and the pennies. At the end of the story, I reached into my wallet, pulled out some money, gave it to him and said, "This is from Emma. It isn't much, but maybe it will help." We prayed together as the train pulled into Penn Station, asking God to bless and hold him as he assisted the families who had been affected by the tragedy.

That Christmas, I received a letter from him. Of all the donations that arrived, Emma's pennies remained a sign of hope to him through the dark weeks that followed our conversation on the train. "Thank you for Emma's gift," he wrote. "It meant so much to me."

Charity is, of course, love. And reading his letter, I wept. A four-year-old girl's offering made a difference at Ground Zero. She had ministered to one of the ministers.

FORGIVENESS

A couple of days after September 11, I was watching the evening news while setting the dining room table. The top story that night was a tape released by Osama bin Laden praising the attacks on New York and Washington.

My husband and I had been careful to guard Emma from the pictures on television, but she had seen enough to know that some planes had crashed into tall buildings and that people had been killed. While I furtively caught the news, she played in another room. Just as I was getting ready to turn off the set, however, she came into the room. The Osama bin Laden video was being replayed.

She looked at the bearded face on the screen. "Mommy," she asked, "is that the bad man? The bad man who killed people?"

I turned off the set and put her in my lap. "Yes, that is the man who did these bad things. But you know what? That does not make him a bad man. God still loves him and wants him to do good. But he disobeyed God and did bad things."

"Why?" she asked.

I wish I knew, I thought. Whatever lack of understanding I possessed, I had to try to answer her question.

"His heart is full of hate," I offered, "but God wants it to be a heart of love. He did it because of hate."

"Will God change his heart? Can God change it to a heart of love?"

I knew there were no guarantees in this department. But I replied, "We can pray for that. We can pray that God changes his heart."

For the next two or so months, Emma kept her own prayer vigil: "that God would change the bad man's heart." Every night before dinner, she would pray. Every morning as we drove to her preschool, she would ask, "Mommy, has God changed the bad man's heart yet?" And every morning, I carefully explained the doctrine of free will to my four-year-old. "God wants to change his heart, Emma. But we can say no to God. God still loves the bad man no matter what."

And every morning, the same answer came from the car seat, "I'll pray more, Mommy."

Shortly after this, I told the story of Emma's prayer in a sermon. Afterward, a parishioner grabbed my arm and angrily said, "Well, your daughter is a better Christian than I am.

I'm angry. I don't want to forgive. I want to kill Osama bin Laden." Her honesty may have been refreshing, but her theology was deeply disturbing.

Praying for one's enemies is central to the Christian practice of forgiveness. As Emma's prayer reminded me daily, Osama bin Laden, whatever horrible things he had done, was a human being, made in God's image and loved by God. Once, he had been as trusting as the little girl who now prayed for him, loved by his own mother, playing with his friends and learning his letters. What had happened, I wondered, that turned his heart from love to hate, and in the process, corrupted the very image of the one in whose name he claimed to act?

Emma's prayer forced me to remember that, above all else, Christians forgive and trust God to do the impossible. "Forgive us our trespasses as we forgive those who trespass against us," implores the church in the prayer given us by Jesus. Christians forgive not only their friends but their enemies.

As the dean of Duke Divinity School, L. Gregory Jones, writes,

> The Christian practice of forgiveness involves us in a whole way of life, a way that is shaped by an ever-deepening friendship with God and with other people.... Its central goal is to reconcile, to restore communion—with God, with one another, and with the whole creation.[2]

My daughter's persistent prayer made me understand that forgiveness springs from the recognition of the other person's humanity, to allow for the extravagant possibility of friendship

41

between enemies. If we forget that, in Jones's words, "we allow feelings of hatred or bitterness to define and consume our lives, even to our own destruction."[3] In some inexplicable way, in praying for Osama bin Laden, he became familiar to me, less frightening. I no longer glanced away in angry shame when I saw his face. Rather, I began searching his eyes for glimmers of a God whom he had forgotten.

Especially in times of conflict and war, God's people need to practice forgiveness by praying for our enemies. For while the world forgets, we are a people of memory: the memory of our enemies as human beings who are rightly loved by their Creator—even while God grieves their hate-filled hearts and violent acts. As Martin Luther King Jr. once wrote, "Love is the only force capable of transforming an enemy into a friend. We never get rid of an enemy by meeting hate with hate; we get rid of an enemy by getting rid of enmity."[4] Outside of brute force, friendship is the only way to maintain peace. Which do we desire—peace by the sword or peace through God's redemptive friendship?

In the dark days following September 11, nearly every minister I know tried to rouse his or her congregation to pray for the terrorists, Afghanistan, and even Osama bin Laden. As one would sadly report to me, "Forgiveness ain't selling right now." And I thought of the words of Dietrich Bonhoeffer, the German theologian killed in a Nazi prison camp: "Reconciliation and redemption, regeneration and the Holy Spirit, love of enemies, cross and resurrection, life in Christ and Christian discipleship—all these things are so difficult and so remote that we hardly venture any more to speak of them."[5]

Some brave people I knew were trying to speak, but it seemed as if few were listening.

CHILDREN AND THE KINGDOM

Through those difficult weeks, I watched as my four-year-old daughter leaned on the practices of Christian discipleship she had been taught as she tried to make sense of a very bad day—and some very frightening changes in her world. In the process, I witnessed the power of Christian practices of honoring the other, giving charity, and granting forgiveness to inspire faith and give hope. And I discovered that faith practices are not private acts. Rather, what Emma did had public consequences—consequences of friendship, reconciliation, challenge, and hope. What if our national response to September 11 had been shaped by honor, charity, and forgiveness? Is it possible for a people in crisis to reach toward virtue as did my four-year-old?

I know it is idealistic to think that the faith practices of a child have anything to do with public life, foreign policy, or the defeat of terrorism. After all, it is religious faith and not politics. But when it comes to idealism, I side with Jesus: "Let the little children come to me; do not stop them; for it is to such as these that the kingdom of God belongs. Truly I tell you, whoever does not receive the kingdom of God as a little child will never enter it" (Mark 10:14b–15).

Of this passage, New Testament scholar Judith Gundry-Volf remarks, "This claim is striking, for nowhere in Jewish literature are children put forward as models for adults, and in a Greco-Roman setting, comparison with children was highly insulting."[6] Yet here in one of the most enduring stories of Jesus, children are the ones who understand the loving reign of God—not the adult disciples. Jesus' teaching echoes the hope of Isaiah's promise: children lead the kingdom. As Gundry-Volf further states, "Jesus blesses the children who are brought to him and teaches that the reign of God belongs to them."[7]

In the inverted world of kingdom ethics, children receive and lead the way to God's reign. Honoring others? Charity? Forgiveness? Is it all a fairy story? Or a faith story?

In her book *The Religious Potential of the Child,* educator Sofia Cavalleti points out that children have the "capacity to see the invisible" as if "it were more tangible and real than the immediate reality." She suggests that Jesus' parables draw children into deep wonder of God's kingdom, allowing them to "see" the invisible mystery of the City of God more easily than do adults. In simple things, like yeast in bread or the tiny mustard seed, children enter imaginatively into God's "expanded horizon" of love and compassion.[8] Perhaps God's reign belongs to children because they see it so much more clearly than adults.

In the fall of 2001, I began to understand how, in the words of Isaiah, children could lead the way to peace. Through imaginative vision and purposeful faith formation, they can be the bearers of the peaceable kingdom. I began to learn from my own daughter as I heard the words of Jesus anew: "Truly I tell you, unless you change and become like children, you will never enter the kingdom of heaven" (Matt. 18:3). After all, you can't get there if you can't see where you're going.

3

"God Bless America" and "Amazing Grace"

A bout a month after September 11, my adult education class at church was discussing the ways in which Christian practices—things like hospitality, forgiveness, and Sabbath keeping—sustain our lives. One of the participants was intently studying the list of such practices that I had posted in the room.

"You know," she said entering into the conversation, "two of these practices have carried us through the last month."

"Which ones?" I asked her.

"Testimony. Everybody has a story. On the news, at the office, in church. We all keep telling our stories. We are compelled to testify to what we saw that day."

"And the other?"

"The other is singing. People are singing. And they are singing the same two songs: 'God Bless America' and 'Amazing Grace.' I'm not sure why, but maybe those are the only two songs every American knows!"

Although it had not occurred to me before she pointed it out, she was right. From the moment Congress stood on the steps of the Capitol singing "God Bless America" to the strains of "Amazing Grace" sung and played at countless church services, public memorials, and funerals, these two songs framed our days in the aftermath of September 11. On the Internet, a citizen's task force circulated a petition reviving an old idea: to make "God Bless America" our national hymn. Articles and books appeared on the history of "Amazing Grace"—with one book referring to the hymn as "our spiritual national anthem."[1]

But a question nagged me long after my friend's observation: Why these songs? Maybe others failed to notice, but "God Bless America" and "Amazing Grace" are very different songs, written in profoundly different circumstances, and espousing widely divergent theological perspectives. How could these two songs serve interchangeably—in our public practice—as spiritual national anthems?

"God Bless America" and "Amazing Grace" represent a deep tension in American life between inclusive public piety and particular religious faith. Most Americans practice faith from a particular tradition: Protestant, Catholic, Jewish, Buddhist, Muslim, Hindu, whatever. A few, but not many of us, check the survey boxes "none" or "all of the above" when someone asks about our religion. The vast majority of us, however, live in relation to larger traditions, sets of beliefs, and faith practices we either inherit or choose.

As every American knows, despite differences of belief, we need to live and work together in a country where no single religion binds us. Thus, a kind of generalized civic expression of faith, what scholars call civil religion, developed as a way to beseech the Divine in public without offending our fellow citizens. Civic piety is, therefore, intentionally vague theology; and it deifies cultural values drawn from religious traditions that are historically relevant or socially unifying. Typically, the way out of the tensions between particular faith and religious diversity is simple: particular faith is personal; generic piety is public.

Since September 11, 2001, however, an odd thing has happened. The personal-public faith division temporarily dissolved, increasing confusion about the relationship between church and state in our society. "Amazing Grace," for all its popularity, is a deeply particular song, one birthed in eighteenth-century evangelical revivalism, not as a "spiritual" anthem but as a specifically Protestant hymn. Yet people were singing it at Catholic funerals and secular public events. And "God Bless America," contrary to the Internet petition's claim, is not a hymn. It is a show tune, written as a form of patriotic entertainment for a general audience. Despite its relentlessly secular imagery, "God Bless America" was being sung in churches. The singing of both songs, interchangeably and in inappropriate settings, worried me about both the theology espoused in American churches and our cherished national commitments to religious freedom and the separation of church and state.

THE CIVIC VALUES OF "GOD BLESS AMERICA"

Irving Berlin, born Israel Baline in 1888, wrote "God Bless America." The son of Russian immigrant Jews, Berlin spent much of his early life trying to escape the painful poverty and social exclusion of New York's ethnic ghettos. He left home at thirteen, shortly after his father's death, to make his own way in the world. Thus began Berlin's lifelong quest to achieve the American dream of wealth and respectability. And in that quest, like so many other Ellis Island immigrants, Berlin muted his Jewish faith and heritage and replaced it with generalized American ideals of success and prosperity. As his biographer, Laurence Bergreen, points out, "'God Bless America' revealed that patriotism was Irving Berlin's true religion."[2]

Berlin wrote "God Bless America" in 1918 for his military musical, *Yip, Yip, Yaphank,* and reissued it (with some modifications) on the eve of World War II. By the time of the song's second public appearance, Berlin was internationally famous as America's songwriter. He had married a wealthy Roman Catholic heiress, was raising his children, and made a fortune in show business. Although his life had not been easy, Berlin embodied the immigrant's American dream. "God Bless America" is the song of an outsider who has found safety, success, and divine protection in a new land. Beginning on Friday night, November 11, 1938, when Kate Smith belted it out over the CBS radio network, it became America's unofficial national anthem.

If patriotism was Berlin's religion, then "God Bless America" expresses the theological content of his faith. In this short song, God is amorphous: sometimes God is the light equated with liberty, and sometimes God is America herself. Although the words implore (or perhaps demand) a transcendent God to bless America from afar, an imminent God also "stands beside her," placing the Divine Being in a mutual relationship with the land. The landscape is godlike in its beauty, vastness, and diversity. Unlike "Amazing Grace" with its clear references to heaven, there is no future state of eternal bliss with God for the redeemed. God has no need to guide his children *home,* because God's people already inhabit holy territory. You need not go anywhere—you are already there. America is both the Divine Protector and the homeland of the blessed.

It is hard to know how Berlin arrived at these religious conclusions, but these sentiments echo the early American tradition of interpreting the New World as God's New Israel, the promised land of peace, flowing with milk and honey. Berlin's experience of American success may have confirmed for him this venerable American myth. To Irving Berlin, born before the modern nation of Israel came to be, the United States probably seemed a pretty good candidate for the Holy Land.

Berlin also lived during a time of rising aspirations among long-excluded Roman Catholics and Jews to achieve the American dream, which was then characterized as a "melting pot" of cultures. All people could share America's bounty—if they accommodated to the ideals of the larger Protestant-tinctured society. At the height of the song's popularity in the 1950s, sociologist Will Herberg claimed that America's religious center had become "Protestant-Catholic-Jew" insofar as these particular traditions assented to notions of generalized democracy, capitalism, individualism, and manifest destiny.[3]

"God Bless America" also reflects midcentury American spirituality—what Princeton professor Robert Wuthnow, in

49

his book *After Heaven,* calls "dwelling place spirituality."[4] The lyrics are the words of a people—settled, confident, and victorious—living a good life in a good land. The song does not request grace, salvation, or eternal life but asks for continued benefits of goodness in the here and now, a cozily majestic interplay between the landscape and "home sweet home." In the 1950s, it witnessed to the triumph of the civic values associated with American homesteading—values of freedom, liberty, and manifest destiny—that had been affirmed by their recent victory against the evil of Nazism.

As if to reward Berlin for giving musical voice to this mid-century vision of American society and spirituality, in 1954—the same year Congress added the words "under God" to the Pledge of Allegiance—President Eisenhower gave the composer of "God Bless America" the Congressional Gold Medal. And a complete synthesis of Judeo-Christian faith and American nationhood, "piety on the Potomac," as American religious historians sometimes quip, framed the religious experience of that generation of twentieth-century Americans.

THE CHRISTIAN VIRTUES OF "AMAZING GRACE"

For all its popularity in the United States, "Amazing Grace" was not originally an American hymn. It is British. Sometime in 1772, the Reverend John Newton (1725–1807), a Church of England clergyman, wrote the first four verses in the rectory of his country parish of Olney; the fifth was added by someone else in the nineteenth century.

Although a minister in the staid English church, Newton had also been swept up in a massive eighteenth-century religious movement, the Evangelical Revival. Led by the preaching of George Whitefield and John Wesley, English-speaking Protestants in Britain and the American colonies experienced their faith in a new way. Instead of being saved by the waters of infant baptism and living a life of good works, the revivalists urged their listeners to be "born again," to be saved from sin and death in a single moment of spiritual transformation that would be emotionally felt. They shifted faith from intellectual assent in Protestant doctrine to a matter of religious experience. The locus of Protestant conversion dropped eighteen inches: head to heart.

John Newton was both a convert to and a minister of evangelical revivalism. As a young man, after his saintly mother died, he followed his father to sea and tried to make his fortune in the African slave trade. In 1748, during a frightening ocean storm, the rebellious and materialistic Newton became born again. For the next seven years, as he grew in faith and learned the Scriptures, he continued his career in slaving until his conscience so afflicted him that he abandoned his old life and, in 1764, became a minister.

"Amazing Grace" is both Newton's testimony and the musical summation of evangelical Protestantism. The action of the hymn is simple. Trapped by original sin, human beings are blind, wretched, and dead to God. God alone saves sinners through unmerited grace, providing both an abundant life and protection from temptation and evil. Life is like the sea—unpredictable in both its tempests and quiet—yet God, as a good ship's captain, will guide the redeemed safely home to shore. Drawing from Scripture, the theology of the Apostle Paul and of Augustine, the experience of Martin Luther, the perspectives of John Calvin, and the evangelical message of Whitefield and Wesley, "Amazing Grace" is a near-perfect theological expression of experiential Protestantism.

Spiritually, the hymn's disposition is that of thankfulness for God's actions, humility at human inability to do good, and awe at God's mercy in salvation. This is a hymn about human frailty and the wonder of divine love. Although a fifth verse, "When we've been there ten thousand years," adds a note of triumph not present in Newton's original four stanzas, yet even here, the sense of victory is completely dependent on God.

"Amazing Grace" resembles "God Bless America" in its interplay between two characters. Unlike "God Bless America," where the interplay is between God and the nation, here, the action is between God and the penitent sinner. And unlike "God Bless America," it is not a dwelling song. "Amazing Grace" is a pilgrimage anthem or a journey song—a hymn of movement from sin to salvation to final bliss with God. Although it is ultimately an optimistic hymn, it does not begin and end in perfection. Rather, "Amazing Grace" recognizes that something is wrong with the universe and that supernatural forces need to fix it. In effect, it says, "I may not be there yet—but God is guiding my heart home."

As "God Bless America" echoed the spiritual experience of a generation, "Amazing Grace" reflected the ways eighteenth-century American Protestants felt God's mercy and love. Their experience of spiritual freedom meshed with emerging ideas of political freedom—and evangelical religion found a comfortable home in America, a nation of movement and restless seeking. In the United States, "Amazing Grace" expressed both cultural and religious longings. What words could better resonate with colonists and settlers—cut off from traditions of home, family, and nation—than "I once was lost, but now am found"? It is no wonder that Judy Collins's 1960s version of "Amazing Grace" would give voice to the baby boomers, a later generation of restless seekers, who, in many ways, were as displaced as their eighteenth-century forebears. For those Americans born after World War II, "Amazing Grace" replaced "God Bless America" as the soundtrack of their spiritual and political experience.

A NATIONAL HYMN?

When the terrorists attacked on September 11, they struck America's home—the symbolic centers of American political, social, and spiritual values. It is easy to see how "God Bless America," a patriotic song that both divinizes and glorifies the nation would resonate with Americans yet again. After all, what is more lasting than the beauty of the American landscape as a bearer of and witness to our liberty? What is sweeter than home? The attack struck the center of American mythology as the dwelling place of God's chosen people, whose buildings and success stand as a testimony to their belief in God's blessing on their land. I think the terrorists

53

knew—and know—this. From their perspective, destroying the American New Israel, with its Babel-like structures, is a divinely mandated war against idolatry.

Even though I know and appreciate Irving Berlin's story, I must admit that, as a Christian, I have a difficult time singing "God Bless America." For it is biblically wrong to equate any secular real estate with God's kingdom. The equation of our land with God's Land has led to a host of problems in American history—including the genocide of native peoples and our abuse of the natural environment. If we see ourselves as divinely guided, a New World Israel, we have given ourselves biblical permission to do as we please, citing ourselves as special, confident in our own salvation.

The great irony and pain of American history is our myth of divine exceptionalism, of being a redeemer nation, set so perfectly to music in "God Bless America." In their recent book, *Captain America and the Crusade Against Evil,* Robert Jewett and John Shelton Lawrence refer to this tendency as "zealous nationalism," that "seeks to redeem the world by destroying enemies."[5] The ironic aspect is that in a nation where Christianity has flourished, this myth has undermined the Christian message of salvation through God's love and justice in the cross. Redemption is not a matter of human will, moral purity, or military might; redemption is the free gift of a suffering and bleeding God. In the Christian story, everyone—and every nation—stands in need of God's redemption. And the Bible itself teaches that no one, apart from God's action, is holy. Much of American public religion, however, interprets our nation as good, pure, innocent, and morally upright—and our enemies as evil. In effect, we have placed ourselves above the Scripture's assessment of the human problem of sinfulness. We substituted gospel humility with national hubris. Be like us Americans, or "be with us," as President Bush himself said in public addresses after September 11, if you want to be saved. And pride, whether personal or national, according to St. Augustine, is not a sign of righteousness. Rather, it reveals a persistent spiritual resistance to the grace of God.

"Amazing Grace" does a much better job with Christian theology—expressing the biblical faith of a humble, contrite people dependent on a merciful God. But I have an almost equally difficult time nominating "Amazing Grace" as a national hymn. It is an individualistic song of religious experience—there's really nothing national about it because it was never meant to be anything more than one person's testimony. Although Newton and his eighteenth-century evangelical friends knew that spiritual transformation led to working on behalf of the poor and oppressed, as demonstrated by their rejection of slavery, "Amazing Grace" is not entirely clear about the public consequences of Christian faith. There is an escapist quality about the hymn that makes me uncomfortable. In the fall of 2001, it may have expressed little more than our sadness, our yearning hope that God's grace enfolded those who so unexpectedly met their deaths. It may well be that the two songs combined, the zealous nationalism of "God Bless America" and the grieving hopefulness of "Amazing Grace," spoke to our anger and pain. But neither hymn—singly or in combination—represented an adequate Christian response to the troubling issues raised by terrorism.

Although I shy away from the idea of a national hymn—
after all, what hymn can truly express the faith of an entire
nation?—the idea of a hymn that sums up the theology of our
uncertain current era intrigues me because singing is such a
powerful practice of community and wholeness. If I were to
pick such a hymn, my choice would be the much less widely known "All My Hope on God Is Founded":

> All my hope on God is founded;
> He doth still my trust renew,
> Me through change and chance he guideth,
> Only good and only true.
> God unknown, he alone,
> Calls my heart to be his own.
>
> Mortal pride and earthly glory,
> Sword and crown betray our trust;
> Though with care and toil we build them,
> Tower and temple turn to dust.
> But God's power, hour by hour,
> Is my temple and my tower.
>
> God's great goodness e'er endureth,
> Deep his wisdom passing thought:
> Splendor, light, and life attend him,
> Beauty springeth out of nought.
> Evermore, from his store,
> Newborn worlds rise and adore.
>
> Still from earth to God eternal
> Sacrifice of praise be done,
> High above all praises praising

For the gift of Christ, his Son.
Christ doth call one and all:
Ye who follow shall not fall.[6]

When I sang "All My Hope" in a church service on September 14, I could barely choke out the line "Tower and temple turn to dust." *Here,* I thought through my tears, *is a hymn that gives voice to the Christian vision of a post–September 11 world.* It expresses both personal and communal humility. And it recognizes the fundamental nature of being at war with terrorists—everything is chaotic. "Sword and crown" cannot, no matter how much we hope, save us. In a capricious universe, God alone is hope and refuge. And yet in the middle of destruction and human anguish, God still gifts the world with the beauty of new creation. This hymn holds out the larger hope for a realm of love and justice on earth—and the strength for God's people to follow the way to that kingdom.

My choice, however, is only for a *Christian* national hymn. With its clear dependence on Christ, "All My Hope" is most appropriate for the 80 to 85 percent of us who claim the Christian tradition. Besides a Christian national hymn, perhaps we need a Buddhist national chant, a Jewish national *shabbat,* an Islamic national fast. Perhaps it is overly idealistic, but maybe—just maybe—if we can be companions in our practices of faith, cherishing and sharing about our real differences, and willing to talk about them in public, our civic piety would be deepened. When we really know what we believe and practice, then together we could call upon a robust God—a God with many names and varied attributes, the One who fills all peoples with grace, mercy, and love and can sustain us through these chaotic and fearful times.

In such days, the witness of particularity in unity would truly be, as Puritan founder John Winthrop hoped for America, "a model of Christian charity" that would stand as "a city set upon a hill, a light for all the nations."[7]

4

Going to the Chapel

For weeks following the attacks, Christ Church in Alexandria, Virginia, offered several prayer services each day—putting a huge strain on the clergy staff. As a result, a few of the lay staff were enlisted for duties typically reserved for the ordained. One Friday, I volunteered to lead morning prayer, a meditative service in the Episcopal tradition.

I arrived at the church very early, right after dawn. As I entered the churchyard, I noticed a well-dressed man was already there. He looked like any other Washington white-collar worker—clothed in Brooks Brothers navy with a briefcase at his side. Only this man was sitting on a grave, weeping. I walked up to him, sat next to him on the centuries-old tomb, and put my arms around the sobbing stranger. His head fell onto my shoulder and he asked a single question: "Why?"

I didn't know how to answer. Finally, breaking the pain-filled quiet, I asked him to go inside with me and pray. In the next few minutes, about ten people joined us as we began the day with the Psalmist's ancient words: "I was glad when they said to me, 'Let us go to the house of the Lord'" (Ps. 122:1).

I never saw him again. He was one of hundreds, maybe even thousands, of people who went to the church in those weeks. At Christ Church, and in congregations across the country, people packed the pews. Ministers and journalists alike were amazed at the size of the crowds. Normal Sunday church attendance in the United States ranges from 30 to 40 percent of the population—high for a Western nation—but in the weeks following the terrorist attacks, it soared. Throughout September 2001, evangelists and television preachers confidently predicted the beginning of a new revival, a millennial Great Awakening, a harbinger of Jesus' return.

By the end of October, however, the crowds had thinned. And by Thanksgiving, attendance had returned to regular levels. A seasoned journalist, who is both a friend and a preacher's son, remarked to me, "Well, the blip is over. I guess people are trying to get back to normal. Odd, though, that so few stayed in church."

For months, his comment stayed with me. Why *did* so many people go to church and not come back?

Many ministers and church leaders blamed it on the quality of the newcomers. The "blip" came from the "no atheists in foxholes" factor—initially, people were scared and sad; but as weeks wore on, their fear abated and their need for comfort decreased. "We didn't have room for all those new people, anyway," said one venerable churchgoer within my earshot. A few optimistically opined that the church, serving as a comfort to those in distress, had accomplished its rescue-operation mission and could now, like the rest of society, try to get back to normal. "We were there," remarked one clergy acquaintance with a sense of spiritual accomplishment, "for those who needed us when they needed us. That's what church is for."

But, I wondered, *don't Christians believe that everybody needs the church?* Not on an ad hoc basis, not only in emergency situations, but as the heart of all that is good and beautiful and true? Does not the church, as Orthodox theologian Alexander Schmemann wrote, exist "for the life of the world"?[1] I was less inclined to blame the comfort-seeking visitors for failing to return than I was beginning to wonder if American churches had somehow failed those who were looking for answers.

Certainly, comforting those who mourn is a biblically appropriate ministry for God's people—reflecting Jesus' own words in Matthew (5:4), "Blessed are they that mourn: for they shall be comforted." Indeed, in those weeks, I realized I had been spiritually "drafted" as a chaplain, a sort of religious rescue worker—praying, holding hands, listening to all those who needed the shoulder of solace.

But as days and weeks went by, I observed that we were not comforting solely with the gospel. Much of the comfort provided by American churches mixed the symbols of church and state, juxtaposing Psalm 23 with the national anthem, carrying both cross and the American flag in processions and rituals. One seminary student of mine reported that, in a church he visited on September 16, the priest himself had carried the American flag and planted it next to the altar. Having done so, the minister turned to the congregation and said, "This flag stays here until this thing is over. And if you don't like it, you are in the wrong church."

This admixture of faith and nation may have comforted some churchgoers (although my student friend quickly decided he was in the wrong church and left!). However, it failed to communicate a biblical vision of church, the transethnic and transnational global community that embraces all people and embodies God's reign of forgiveness and reconciliation. Nor did it clearly show God's people responding to the crisis with spiritual maturity, biblical wisdom, or theological insight. By waving flags and singing patriotic songs, many churches functioned as national chapels in the days following September 11 and the warring days that followed.

For much of American religious history, mainline Protestant churches understood themselves as a kind of unofficial national religion, an informal and multidenominational establishment. Although the state could not legally establish a particular faith, in practice, the state "preferred" a generic form of Protestantism in its culture and laws. Protestant Bible reading and prayers were offered in public schools; only Protestant chaplains served the military and government; and Protestant morals about work, family, alcohol, and sexuality shaped politics. Returning the favor of state privilege, Protestant churches instituted religious services blessing secular holidays—such as Thanksgiving, Veterans Day, and Independence Day. A graduate school professor once remarked to me that the friendly interplay of American government and Protestant religion was a more like a "picket fence of separation" than a wall.

Established religions, whether they are formally or informally constructed, serve to comfort and bless society; they function as chapels. They baptize a nation's ideals and practices by proclaiming divine guidance and support. They take care of people's needs. Established religions, like chapels, challenge neither adherents nor society.

Historically, mainline Protestants had so blurred the line between state and church that it has taken nearly a century of legislation and judicial opinion to try to define exactly what the framers of the Constitution meant by "no law respecting an establishment of religion." Sociologists argue that the disestablishment of American Protestantism actually happened in three stages: constitutionally in 1789; by being challenged through religious pluralism by Catholics and Jews in the late nineteenth century; and through the cultural rejection of traditional religious authorities in the 1960s.

Through this long process, by the 1990s, many American congregations had finally begun to understand the ramifications of the separation of church and state—that the government would not and could not sponsor, support, propagate, or even prefer their religious views. Many mainline Protestants had begun to see themselves as "culturally marginalized" in a "post-Protestant" society.[2] But the sense of civic duty, of patriotic religiosity, was so entrenched in the psyche of these churches that many congregations fell back into their historic default position of being civil chapels when confronted with a national emergency.

63

Not surprisingly, people went to church following September 11 seeking comfort, a natural urge in times of distress. They sought the consolation of chapel religion. From much of what I have read, heard, and witnessed, American churches provided just that. We bound up the wounds of the brokenhearted. But there is a problem with this kind of chapel: it is optional. You only go when you need it; when you want a blessing or prayer; when you want to get married, baptize your children, or bury your parents. When you are sad or sick. When you go off to war. When you want to feel God is on your side. The Sunday after the attacks, churches offered plenty of chapel religion.

But I wondered: *How many embodied the church?* How many witnessed to their citizenship in another city, the "city that has foundations, whose architect and builder is God" (Heb. 11:10)? We might comfort the earthly city, but were we proclaiming the city of God?

CHAPEL AS OPTIONAL

Americans have perfected the type of optional chapel religion that has given us hospital chapels, wedding chapels, drive-through chapels, airport chapels, cruise ship chapels, funeral chapels, chapels of ease, and nondenominational congregations of thousands called "chapels." We did not, of course, invent chapel. Rather, Americans inherited it from our European forebears.

The word *chapel* originated in the military. French kings housed the cape (late Latin, *cappella,* diminutive of *cappa*) of their patron saint, Martin of Tours, in a temporary structure that they carried into battle as a holy relic to ensure victory over their enemies. St. Martin of Tours (d. 397), the son of pagan parents, converted to the Christian faith as a young man. Although early Christians believed it was immoral to serve in the military, Martin's father forced him to join the Roman army and become a soldier for Caesar.

According to legend, when the devout Martin was still a catechumen (not yet a full member of the church), he gave half of his military cloak to a beggar, literally following Jesus' teaching to give one's coat to the poor. That night, Jesus appeared to Martin in a dream, saying, "Martin, a simple catechumen covered me with this garment." When this episode became public knowledge, the cape was rumored to have miraculous powers. Eventually, French rulers claimed to possess the cape as a relic and used it to ensure military victory against their enemies. They housed it in a portable chapel that could be carried into battle, and it was served by priests known as chaplains.

Both the words *chapel* and *chaplain* derive from the story of the reluctant soldier-convert whose cape became a battlefield relic. In general usage, the word *chapel* came to mean, as stated in the *Oxford Dictionary of the Christian Church,* "a variety of buildings which in various ways were less than churches."

Chapels are buildings where one can expect to find a chaplain, a person who helps the supplicant find spiritual assurance. Chaplains comfort in crisis, bless state functions, or provide religious life rituals on an occasional basis to temporary congregations. One of the traditional names for these congregations is "chapel of ease" indicating that chapels are intended to make it easy for people to attend. By its very nature, chapel is low-demand religion. Attendees decide what religious services they want and when—and patronize the chapel at their own need or convenience. Chapel is optional. And it is not reciprocal. You do not have to give anything back or be part of the community. A friend of mine calls it "church lite."

Throughout much of American history, mainline Protestant churches functioned as national chapels. As sociologists of religion Roger Finke and Rodney Stark point out in their book, *The Churching of America,* traditional mainline churches consistently "de-sacralized" themselves by accommodating secular culture.[3] Their churches eventually became indistinguishable both from each other and from some generalized, vaguely religious form of middle-class American values, essentially chapels of ease for a large swath of the populace. For decades, a broadly Protestant form of theology, prayer, and liturgy grounded civic occasions; and mainline ministers provided religious services to public schools and colleges, the military, state houses, and the Congress. Before the 1960s, most Protestants expected their churches to baptize the public order—to support American values, bless the state's actions, pray for national officials, celebrate national holidays, display its flag in their sanctuaries, march with its armies, and commemorate the state's martyrs. In American Protestant Christendom, a world that was dying about the time I was born, the words *church* and *chapel* were basically interchangeable.

Eventually, mainline Protestant accommodation to American culture fostered a kind of religious ennui among those looking for more robust faiths. Between 1960 and 2000, near-ly an entire generation of Americans abandoned the mainline chapels that were their birthright. Forty years separated the vanished world of comfortable Protestant piety and contem-porary secular pluralism. On September 11, 2001, however, some ancestral impulse seized the populace as even unchurched citizens flocked to those old mainline churches seeking the comfort of St. Martin's cape—or our national equivalent, the American flag.

Like St. Martin, those of us serving at Christ Church wrapped them in its protective folds. We gave comfort and shelter. And when folks felt warm enough, they left and did not return.

THE BODY OF CHRIST

There is nothing wrong with offering shelter to strangers in the midst of war. Indeed, that is one of the most venerable practices of Christian faith. And chapels serve an important function in relation to the church, a kind of spiritual outpost to those beyond reach of a traditional congregation.

A problem arises, however, when people expect that chapel services are the entirety of church. By offering low-demand religion for much of the twentieth century, mainline congregations reinforced the idea that church was, essentially, a place of comfort: chapel. The church is a building one goes to when in need of spiritual assistance. Many congregations limit themselves to these cultural expectations. After September 11, when churches defaulted back to being state chapels, they missed the opportunity of a generation—to be church.

Church is much more than chapel. Whereas *chapel* is defined statically as a structure (or a part of a structure), the term for *church* is dynamic and organic: the *ecclesia,* the Greek word meaning gathering, assembly, or congregation.

Early Christians never defined *church* as a building. Rather, *they* were church; they were the body of Jesus Christ. In his letters, the Apostle Paul described the Christian assembly as a body, and he reminded believers that "You are the temple of the Holy Spirit" and "the Bride of Christ." The church was not, as it would become later, a voluntary association made up of members. Rather, it was a relational community reflecting God's reign, established by Jesus Christ, birthed in the waters of baptism, fed with the bread and wine of the Eucharist, and nurtured by practices of faith. Church is not a place you go; church is not a club you join; church is something you are.

Christians have often lost this dynamic sense of who and what they are and have redefined church variously as an institution, a magisterium, a building, or a denomination. In the mid-twentieth century, however, Catholic and Protestant theologians began to recover the vision of church as body (rather than as building or institution). For Catholics, Vatican II rearticulated this early Christian understanding. In 1982, the Protestant World Council of Churches urged a return to the New Testament's theological ideal: "In a broken world God calls the whole of humanity to become God's people . . . Belonging to the Church means living in communion with God through Jesus Christ in the Holy Spirit. . . . The Church is called to proclaim and prefigure the Kingdom of God."[4]

In the weeks following September 11, I wondered whether congregations had finally begun to understand the ramifications of the separation of church and state. Had visitors glimpsed the *ecclesia* of God's people—the understanding of church making its way anew through our communities—of those in living communion with God, proclaiming and prefiguring the kingdom? Did the newcomers, those who were mourning, see or sense the power of God in the congregations they visited? I became increasingly skeptical that they could. I was having a hard time either seeing or sensing it from where I sat at Christ Church in Alexandria.

CHURCH OR CHAPEL?

The histories of Christ Church in Alexandria, Virginia, and St. Paul's Chapel in New York City intertwine. Although separated geographically, the colonial buildings resemble each other; they both date from the 1760s, and both claim the honor of having George Washington as a regular worshiper. Each radiates a museum's quiet serenity. Each proudly marks the pew once occupied by the nation's first president.

Beside their eighteenth-century claims to fame, Christ Church and St. Paul's also share a more recent historical event—both were perilously close to the violence of September 11. Christ Church sits four miles from the Pentagon, and St. Paul's is across the street from the World Trade Center. The crisis of September 11 brought each to a crossroads of church and chapel.

69

Although Christ Church was founded as a parish church, the tension between *ecclesia* and chapel is a long one in Alexandria. During the Civil War, the Yankees turned most Virginia churches into barns or hospitals. Not Christ Church, however. In 1861, the Union officers occupying Alexandria were impressed that Washington was once a member of the congregation. They appropriated Christ Church as their own private military chapel.

The townsfolk, unhappy with the Yankee invaders, left to worship at home or with other congregations. After the war, they wanted their building back. But the army officers wanted to stay. The bishop negotiated a settlement and united the two groups into a single congregation. By the late nineteenth century, the church marked its dual heritage by emphasizing a common culture of military duty that honored its two most famous parishioners, Washington and Robert E. Lee, with large memorials framing the chancel.

Most people think Christ Church embodies the eighteenth century. However, the church's symbolic universe, complete with Washington and Lee, was actually crafted in the late nineteenth century and reflects the worldview of that later time. After the war, the parish essentially remade Washington and Lee into romantic heroes of American liberty and Christian patriotism. During the post–Civil War period, mainline Protestants believed, according to historian George Marsden, "that the world's destiny lay with the Anglo-Saxon race," and that a "love of liberty and a 'pure spiritual Christianity'" were America's gifts to the world.[5] In post–Civil War culture, Washington and Lee served as exemplars of these American virtues, saints of an American cultus. Christ

Church's architecture bespeaks that reality—not the one of the older, eighteenth-century Anglican village church.

From its founding in 1767 until the Civil War, Christ Church was able to adjust to changing cultural circumstances, to social and theological crises of all sorts. After the Civil War, for whatever reason, the church froze around the ideals of late nineteenth-century white Protestantism, which, according to Marsden, "thoroughly blended dominant American secular and religious goals."[6] With the addition of Lee to its pantheon, Christ Church spoke this language of American faith with a Virginia accent.

Guided by Washington and Lee, each successive generation at Christ Church recrafted the congregational culture of Americanism and piety. Along the way, they adjusted to Wilsonian democracy, the New Deal, anti-Communism, and the Great Society. But its fundamental sense of identity as a chapel of the state has never substantially changed.

The cultural glue for all this at Christ Church is unquestioned acceptance of soldiering as a way of life. Unlike St. Martin and the early followers of Jesus, who saw a fundamental tension between Christian discipleship and the military, Christ Church seemed unable to recognize that such a tension may exist. For many, the year's liturgical high point is the Veterans Day service. Each November, parishioners paper an entire wall of the parish house (about forty feet long and twelve feet high) with their own military photographs and commemorate their service to God and country. As it was in the late nineteenth century, so it was in the late twentieth. The church thoroughly blended American secular and Christian religious goals.

Being a good soldier, a good American, and a good Christian are of a piece.

In the 1980s and 1990s, many new people joined the church—primarily baby-boomer seekers and returnees—some of whom looked askance at the blending. Christ Church's Christianized manifest destiny and its military "glue" seemed the stuff of another generation. If you wanted to, you could ignore it.

With September 11, however, it could no longer be ignored. Distraught parishioners laid siege to the clergy. As comfort, they wanted familiar church and familiar liturgy. They insisted upon a military color guard, wanted to sing the national anthem, drape the sanctuary with bunting, and play taps to close the upcoming Sunday service. With some trepidation, the clergy nixed the color guard, bunting, and taps and compromised with "America the Beautiful." The rector preached a stunning sermon comparing the church to a "gilded hearse" and urged, "This is not the time for playing church. *No more play church.*" Some people thought it was a great sermon, but I heard a lot of grumbling too. What was he talking about? Play church? Why wasn't he preaching on God's power and American victory?

No matter what the clergy thought or some spiritually mature congregants tried to do, the church's identity of state chapel completely took over. It was as if the building had a life and will of its own. Within a week, the property was covered with flags—including one the size of a barn. On Veterans Day, the commander of the USS *Cole,* the ship bombed months earlier in Yemen, delivered the address. Their eyes brimming with tears, the audience cheered and toasted him with champagne—surrounded by pictures of themselves in uniform hanging on the wall. The gift shop volunteers filled their store with patriotic knickknacks. Parishioners stuffed clear glass Christmas tree ornaments with tiny American flags and red, blue, and silver sparkles to sell as a fundraiser.

From the way some people acted, and from snippets of conversation I overheard, it appeared that many congregants interpreted the terrorist attacks as if we were back in World War II. For them, the world was once again divided into good and evil, and America was on a great military crusade to destroy the evildoers. Setting out the knickknacks or preparing the Christmas ornaments was like knitting socks for soldiers at the front or planting a victory garden in the backyard. One woman even suggested that we use some church space to have a USO canteen—"just like we did in the old days." Although it came violently and unexpectedly, some congregants seemed happily nostalgic about this new-old, black-and-white world as they easily equated Osama bin Laden with Adolf Hitler. Just as with World War II, their lives had purpose and a cause. And it wasn't just those who lived through World War II; younger members, eager for a quick end to the terrorist threat, jumped on the patriotic bandwagon too. They could be part of a valiant quest: redeeming the world through American goodness and democracy.

If it hadn't been so passionate, it might have seemed a little corny to me. But I could, oddly enough, sympathize. I felt angry and afraid and longed for peace and security. I too want my life to have meaning. I understand the longing for giving oneself to a heroic quest. Between me and those longings, however, stood all kinds of complicating factors: things like nuclear warfare, the painful political revelations of Watergate, the emergence of global fundamentalisms. Osama bin Laden was not Adolf Hitler. However twisted he was, Hitler was a western European, a person whose ideas borrowed from and perverted Western philosophy and Christianity. We could, when we really tried, understand him and the darkness that drove him.

But Osama bin Laden? Al Qaeda? This was something entirely foreign, something we could barely comprehend. It had to do with globalization and cultural anxiety, with Western economic imperialism and the erosion of tradition in ancient societies. It reached back to the challenge Mohammed first issued to Christianity in the seventh century, back to the carnage of the medieval Crusades. In my historical imagination, I heard the great Pope Urban II preaching the First Crusade in 1095. The good Christian to whom he preached shouted back: "God wills it!" When they took Jerusalem five years later, the holy knights praised God for their great victory as they walked ankle-deep through the blood of the Muslims and Jews they had slaughtered. It may have felt black-and-white for many Americans, but it wasn't. I thought of theologian Reinhold Niebuhr's insistence that all nations, all political systems, and all rulers sin and fail to do God's justice.

But in many ways, the complexities may have proved too big a challenge for people angry and sad over the terrorist attacks. They wanted to do something. Something to help. And they did what they did the last time their world felt threatened—they waved flags and knitted socks. They readied themselves for war.

This may have comforted some people, but it did not seem like church to me. I kept thinking of a hopeful line from Stanley Hauerwas about the church: "In a fragmented world that is a world perpetually at war, Christians can again recover how exciting and exhilarating it is to be a people of peace."[7] Although I could not answer the stranger in the churchyard on the morning he asked the question, the why of September 11, the why of life is belonging to such an exciting and exhilarating people, of being emissaries from that other city. That gives life meaning. Recovering Christian faith as a distinctive way of life is a heroic quest, a journey that is about goodness and beauty and peace.

That distinctive way of life kept trying to break through Christ Church's prominently displayed patriotic Protestant-ism—in prayer groups and in adult study groups, through outreach and mission concerns. One stunning example of parishioners trying to be the church happened weekly in the church's basement. At the time of the terrorist attacks and after, a small group of parishioners taught English to a large number of Muslim women and their children. There, deep under the flag-draped gift shop, Christians helped Muslim immigrants. However, those Muslim women had to walk past doors covered with the United We Stand signs. I wondered what the immigrant women thought about all the flag wav-ing and, eventually, the war in Afghanistan. What did they see in us? Did they see us worshiping Jesus the loving Son of God, the savior of all peoples? Or was he obscured by the church's zealous nationalism?

As I watched the women descend to their classrooms in the basement, I thought of the friendships that had formed between teachers and students. Up here, street level, flags waved, and good Christian soldiers went off to war. Down there, Christ's people humbly served the strangers among us. I recalled that the earliest Christians held their services in the catacombs. *Maybe,* I mused, *real church is always underground.*

Back upstairs, a tense level of unspoken conflict continued to strain the congregation. One grateful parishioner presented the rector with a stained-glass window of the American flag in thanks for his support of the church's patriotic fervor. In December, adult education offered a class on peacemaking as a practice of faith. A surprising number of congregants came and were willing to listen, discuss, and engage difficult issues. We recruited the children to make peace banners. But in those weeks, I heard little else of peace. I mostly heard the beating drums of revenge and war, sorrowful sobs over the loss of American power. I heard the blending of American policy and religious language. Those of us upset by the confusion between state and church were effectively silenced. It seemed a little dangerous to dream of peace, to be citizens of another city.

In New York, however, some of my friends and colleagues experienced September 11 in a different way. They served at the rescue center at St. Paul's Chapel. There, a tiny building, whose best days were long past, found itself at Ground Zero, one of the few structures still standing.

I knew St. Paul's Chapel. In summer 1998, I did research at the New York Public Library on nineteenth-century Episcopal women. While reading some papers, I discovered that one of these women had been a member of St. Paul's and, in 1800 and 1804, had buried her infant children in its churchyard. Her sad diary touched me. I left the library, hailed a taxi, and went to find the graves.

When I arrived at St. Paul's, the chapel was locked behind huge iron gates—only open scant hours for an occasional service or tourist. Undaunted, I walked several blocks to its mother church, Trinity Wall Street, fetched a verger, and asked to be let in to St. Paul's.

The chapel was empty—it nearly always was. Trinity was contemplating what to do with the building. *A dead church,* I thought as I followed the verger in. A pamphlet informed me that since Washington's 1789 inauguration, a few "important" events had occurred there—notably "the oil painting of the Great Seal of the United States (hanging above the Washington pew) was loaned to Independence Hall" in 1963.

On display was an exhibit titled "It Is Done." Although the title referred to the first president's inauguration, it echoed Jesus' words from the cross: "It is finished" (John 19:30). *A fitting epitaph for the place,* I mused. I went outside and stood in the churchyard, at the spot I knew to be the unmarked graves of babies who died two hundred years ago, and looked back at the church. St. Paul's was a beautiful building. But it was surely done. This ghostly temple—caught in the crucible of its glorious past and empty pews—might be the future of mainline church. A museum. Not a church. Hardly even a chapel.

On September 11, St. Paul's proved it was not done. And that the cross does, sometimes even in this life, lead to resurrection. Indeed, it stood while modern buildings fell and as the dust of the newly dead rained down into its ancient graveyard. Following the attacks, some authorities wanted to close it, but others envisioned St. Paul's with a new mission—to serve the rescue workers at the World Trade Center site.

For eight months, hundreds of volunteers worked twelve-hour shifts ministering to firefighters, construction workers, police, and recovery personnel. There were American flags, but huge, colorful banners reading "Peace," "Grace," "Courage," and "Oklahoma City Loves You" also hung from the balconies. Flowers, cards, icons, crosses, and schoolchildren's drawings decorated the sanctuary. St. Paul's offered prayer, counseling, and music; lunch, back massage, and a foot clinic.

St. Paul's Chapel, once a chapel of ease, became anything but easy. The volunteers discovered the hard joy of compassion, and they embodied the paradoxical lightness of God's yoke. The once-hushed colonial building threw its doors open. People cried, ate, and slept in the sanctuary. The church served anyone and everyone as Jesus Christ would have served.

Of it, one volunteer named Jan W. wrote, "I saw the church in a new light this week!"

> I am a cradle Episcopalian and have never seen the church be anything but a pristine house of worship, as I had always envisioned it to be. But this week, at St. Paul's Chapel, I saw the church in its most beautiful form . . . as a sanctuary for those in need; as a HOME, not just a house, of God. . . . The walls, pillars, doors all

exclaim God's love and the wonder of people throughout the world whose faith is strong in the face of such horror. It was awe-inspiring. It changed me. And it changed my definition of a church.[8]

The Reverend Dr. Fred Burnham, who was then director of Trinity Institute, served hundreds of hours at St. Paul's and found the "meaning of 9-11" there. "At St. Paul's," he recalls, "I found a community of compassion, where all the people who came there had in some way experienced radical vulnerability on September 11 and were coming with a purpose: to be compassionate, to be there for others in need. It was . . . [a] foretaste of the kingdom. Out of this tragedy the kind of personal transformation can take place that ultimately can be a kernel out of which some real transformation of human relations can take place across the globe."[9]

Church, of which Jan and Fred write, is not like chapel. It is not optional. But it is not required, either. Like grace, it is irresistible. It is so powerful that it keeps pulling you back. You cannot resist it. It changes you. You meet God. The universe turns inside out. Church, the body of Jesus Christ, becomes the grounding point of all of life. You go and keep on going. As the Psalmist exclaims, "How lovely is your dwelling place, O Lord of hosts! My soul longs, indeed it faints for the courts of the Lord. . . . For a day in your courts is better than a thousand elsewhere. I would rather be a doorkeeper in the house of my God than live in the tents of wickedness" (Ps. 84:1, 2, 10).

Living Christianity is high-demand faith. Once experienced, it is hard to ever forget. It gets under your skin. You cannot ever leave. You are home.

The stories of Christ Church and St. Paul's are not spiritual morality tales of bad church versus good church. Rather, they communicate something of the tension and texture of the choices and challenges that thousands of congregations across the country faced on September 11. They tell us about the history of mainline congregations and about the future.

To find comfort, Christ Church reached back to its establishment past, a time of Anglo-Saxon empire when mainline Protestantism served as chaplain to the nation, back to World War II when things seemed so much clearer and less complex. For Christ Church, it was a natural and visceral response, one fostered by the symbolic power of its building, its romanticized history, and its staid liturgy. Reaching back was a way of retelling its own story that strengthened congregational resolve. The parish reaffirmed its historic identity as established religion, a kind of national chapel, to get through the crisis. Chapel is about blessing what is, about comfort in the midst of fear, about victory for our side. Chapel is about us.

I, however, am convinced that Americans can no longer afford chapel religion. In the face of global terrorism and religious fundamentalisms, chapel is deeply inadequate. In the weeks after September 11, the people at Christ Church kept asking a single question: "Why?" We never really answered that question. We offered an old way of coping through the priestly style of civic piety. I think people sensed that old-fashioned patriotic Protestantism could not answer their questions or give meaning in this strange new world.

Although Christ Church's faith may have been meaningful for nineteenth- and twentieth-century people, it seemed largely incapable of addressing the violent arrival of this new millennium on a bright September morning. There was no room in that older world for national sin and forgiveness; for the cruelties and conflicts of history; for insurgent fundamentalism and religious pluralism; for the interconnected global responsibilities of justice and injustice; for humility, suffering, and defeat. As I embraced those who came to Christ Church and then watched them leave, I dreamed of something else, something beyond the niceties of mainline American piety. I kept praying that a new kind of church might be birthed in the darkness of the days.

Devotional writer Vance Havner once said, "God sometimes snuffs out our brightest candle that we may look up to his eternal stars."[10] September 11, 2001, snuffed out old St. Paul's only to revive it in a new way. That new way was a challenging vision of God's reign—of what can be—and a lived expression of prophetic civic faith. In his book *9-11: Meditation at the Center of the World,* Eugene Kennedy writes of what he learned at Ground Zero: "We are the senses of the galaxies, called to recognize their pain in our own and to feel it on behalf of all being. We stand together as the chorus of the universe, singing in our suffering of all suffering and its healing through love. Our vocation is to see that no one suffers alone, that no pain goes unnoticed, and none is without meaning. We are the medium through which the cosmos feels its heartbreak but also the mediators of its comfort and resurrection."[11] Things had been dark for a long time at St. Paul's, but after September 11, those who were there could finally see God's stars. They could dream of what might be.

In the pain and fear of September 11, Christ Church sought comfort by relighting candles of priestly civil religion. Some evening, when you go on a historical tour of Alexandria, visit Christ Church. By candlelight, it is beautiful. It looks just as it did a century ago. An inviting chapel, warm and embracing. As it has when facing crises of generations past, Christ Church continues to glow by the light of its candles. But the earthly candles' gentle flickers obscured God's galaxies pulsating with luminous love. Some churches soared to the stars in the past two years. Other than St. Paul's, I do not know their names or where they are. But I can imagine what they are like, and they are not softly lit chapels. Church is about transformation: God changes us through the compassionate hospitality of love. Church is an encounter with a reality only distantly perceived in other parts of life, the place where the veil between earth and heaven is rent, and where, through each other, we can finally touch God. Chapel is about controlling the disorder, about making religion easy. Church is never easy the way chapel can be. Church is about the kind of comfort that makes God's people fearless comforters. Chapel is about what is. Church is about entering into divine chaos, trembling with fear and vulnerability, and finding—at the edges of the universe—God's suffering, reconciling love.

And I kept wondering: instead of singing "America the Beautiful" to guide us through the dark days, what if we had looked up and caught a glimpse of God's eternal stars? What if Christian communities had been church and not chapel? What if we had been prophets instead of priests?

5

Compassionate Imperialism?

In September 2002, I was driving my daughter home from preschool and listening to National Public Radio. A commentator was discussing the White House's new national security strategy. According to members of the administration, "we," that is, the United States, reserved the right of acting preemptively against any threat of violence and would maintain unilateral and permanent military superiority.

Permanent military superiority? It sounded ludicrous to me, like a document leaked by some political tyro and never intended to be discussed in public. Preemptive military action? As a person trained as a historian, I actually laughed out loud at the prospect of such a policy succeeding politically in a democracy. The reporter, however, was serious. This national security strategy would go down in history as the Bush doctrine, a radically new understanding of foreign policy and military force. No American president had ever developed such a bold expression of international power.

Indignation quickly replaced my laughter. *They are serious,* I thought. *They are really serious.* And aloud, with only a preschooler to respond, I asked: "What have we become, the Roman Empire?" Politicians—especially liberals—have often used the language of empire as sloganeering. But this national security strategy pointed to something far beyond politicized words. As Michael Ignatieff would write a few months later in the *New York Times Magazine,* "Yet what word but 'empire' describes the awesome thing that America is becoming? . . . [This nation] fills the hearts and minds of an entire planet with its dreams and desires."[1]

Until that day, I thought the rhetoric of imperialism extreme. After all, the United States has always resisted empire. Driving down King Street in the golden-hued sunset that day, I recalled the impossibility of empire—of all the political entities that have come and gone in history that tried to rule the world—especially that of ancient Rome. "Has September 11 driven us," I wondered aloud, "to become the Roman Empire? Have our fears so compelled us?"

Asleep in her car seat, Emma did not answer.

As would become evident in the next few months, the president's empire would not be based, as past European empires had been, upon the extension of "the white man's burden." Rather, he articulated an empire of goodness, democracy, and liberty, what Michael Ignatieff called "Nation Building Lite," ruling benevolently through the will of the people.[2] When the national security strategy combined, however, with the president's religious rhetoric, it sounded to me like Christian Empire Lite. Or maybe not so lite. In the past two years, the president's interests switched—from compassionate conservatism to compassionate imperialism. From a Christian America to a Christian empire.

I felt worried. Whether Christians are running an imperial government or are subject to it, the faith has never fared well at the hands of empire.

EARLY CHRISTIANS AND EMPIRE

In his recent book *Jesus and Empire,* New Testament scholar Richard Horsley argues that Jesus' entire ministry is best understood as a Jewish political protest against Roman imperialism. Far from the hyperspiritualized figure of most American Sunday schools, Jesus was a traitorous prophet who both condemned Roman oppression and "proclaimed and enacted God's renewal of the people in promise of the kingdom's blessings." Horsley further states that the Gospel of Mark represents a "hidden transcript" of peasant resistance to empire, a story that "empowered and emboldened" Jesus' earliest followers to renew their covenant as God's kingdom people. "This mission," Horsley claims, "presents a stark contrast with the Roman imperial order."[3]

Although popular Christianity often assumes that Jews killed Jesus for religious reasons, most contemporary biblical scholars agree that Roman authorities killed Jesus because of his politics. The prophet from Nazareth was stirring up the Jews, giving voice to their longing for a political redeemer to throw off the yoke of imperial oppression and set up God's kingdom on earth. From the Roman point of view, Jesus was a dangerous traitor, a potential threat to their political control of the Jewish Holy Land. As they would any political traitor, the Romans executed him. However, Jesus' message of communal renewal proved so compelling among those whom the empire oppressed that even after Jesus' death, in Horsley's words, "People who were the products of . . . Rome now formed new communities of an alternative social order, the *ecclesiai,* or 'assemblies' of the proto-Christian movement."[4] From the very beginning, the majority of Jesus' followers understood themselves to be citizens of God's city, who repudiated the "militaristic nationalism" of the surrounding culture.[5]

The oppositional politics of early Christian communities form the subtext of much of the New Testament—including the Apostle Paul's supposedly conservative teachings. Throughout his letters, Paul consistently placed the norms of the Roman Empire *against* those of Christian practices. In Romans 12–15, often quoted as Paul's most traditional defense of the social order ("Let every person be subject to the governing authorities," Rom. 13:1), the apostle's larger argument urges Christians to "no longer define themselves" as Roman citizens, but as "sons and daughters of God."[6] Instead of supporting the political order, Paul actually undermined it by borrowing the language of empire and applying it to Jesus, God, and the kingdom—using, for example, Roman terms for Caesar as titles for Christ and God. Indeed, Paul appropriated a host of secular, imperial political terms for Christian purposes: Jesus is Savior, not the emperor. The *gospel,* or the good news, a term once used to describe Caesar's realm of global peace and security, becomes, for Paul, the good news of God's reign of mercy and justice.

Paul's early audience understood the implications of his teachings so well that the venerated apostle would occasionally have to remind them that obeying the law and maintaining some social order could be an effective strategy to evangelize the empire and to protect the young church from persecution. But the Book of Acts depicts the persistent radical nature of early Christianity: "These people who have been turning the world upside down have come here also," complained authorities in Thessalonica, "They are acting contrary to the decrees of the emperor, saying that there is another King named Jesus!" (Acts 17:7). Jesus' earliest followers emulated their Lord by being political outcasts, potential traitors to the Roman Empire.

Early Christians suffered death for their opposition to "the decrees of the Emperor" and their confession of Jesus as Emperor (that is, Lord). Although martyrdom was not as widely spread as many believe, it nevertheless points to a fundamental truth of early Christianity: Christians understood themselves to be a different kind of society, answering to a ruler who was neither human nor earthly. "The communities of the movement," writes Richard Horsley, "constituted alternative values, social relations, and, to a degree, an alternative society to the Roman imperial order. To use an old cliché, they were '*in* but not *of*' the empire."[7]

At its heart, Christianity is an assembly of those who practice Jesus' teaching of God's kingdom, an ethical and social vision that empowered people to resist ancient Roman rule. As Yale historian Rowan Greer admits:

> However sympathetic one may be to early Christianity, it is impossible to avoid the conclusion that persecution was a natural response to it. The Roman world rightly saw that one possible implication of Christianity was a rejection of the social order.[8]

87

Historian David Chidester's assessment is even more pointed: "Opposition to the state was deeply embedded in [Christian] tradition."[9] Plenty of Jesus' followers concluded that they were "another city"—and willingly accepted the consequences of their alternative citizenship and resisted the religious and social norms of Rome. After all, Christian sacred writings identified Rome with the Antichrist! The empire attempted to rid itself of these traitors, those Christians who undermined the Roman military, the Roman family, the traditions of ancient Roman faith, and the political fabric of the empire itself.

THE THIRD FALL

For most American Christians, it is hard to remember a time when Christianity did anything but support the state. Growing up, as I did, in both mainline Methodism and, later, an evangelical Bible church, my ministers taught that good Christians paid taxes, obeyed the government, submitted to all in authority, and proudly served in the military. Although we puzzled about why the Bible never mentioned the United States, our favored biblical interpreters assured us that our nation was blessed by God and would, according to biblical prophecy, defend Christ's cause of freedom, democracy, and individual rights at the Battle of Armageddon against the evils of Soviet empire. We knew this to be true because George Washington, Thomas Jefferson, and all the founding fathers were faithful men and established America as a Christian nation—just as our ministers had taught us.

As a college student, I discovered that none of the religious mythology about America's founding was historically true. And as a graduate student in religious studies, I worked with George Marsden, a prominent Christian historian, who had written explicitly against such patriotic romanticism regarding church and state. Early Americans had been as disturbed as we had been in the Bible church that Scripture did not mention the New World; as people formed by biblical narrative, they fancied themselves a New Israel and fashioned a civic tradition of faith fit for God's people. They intertwined the Christian and Jewish stories with their own and, in the process, created an imaginative legacy of civil mythology that remains a potent part of national identity to this day.

In the wake of September 11, I could appreciate—although not agree with—the rebirth of civil religion, a civic faith emphasizing God's care for America, culturally adapted from earlier days in an attempt to include Muslims, Buddhists, and Hindus along with Christians and Jews. Especially in the dark months immediately following the attacks, love for both God and country made some sense. Even if I did not express it by hanging a flag, I felt it too.

But I had a harder time understanding Christianity and empire and how a president could claim both the right to permanent military superiority and Jesus as his "mentor." Although I try, in charity, to avoid the temptation of judging anyone's faith, I felt pretty sure that if nothing else, the president who promoted the new national security strategy must understand Christian tradition differently than I do. From public speeches and equally public acts, it appeared that President Bush believed that no tension existed between the United States, Christian Scripture and classical theology, and the emergence of an American global empire. And that this nation bears a singular mission of Christian imperialism, as the president himself would claim: "The United States was called to bring God's gift of liberty to 'every human being in the world.'"[10]

How could this be? How could any Christian who reads the New Testament *not* see some contradiction between Jesus and empire, the perils of equating God's cause with the cause of a nation?

When they were a rural, tribal people overseen by wise judges, the ancient Hebrews begged God for a king. God told the Jews it was a bad idea but nevertheless granted their request. For the next several hundred years, they suffered greatly because they conflated faith in God with political nationhood. Yes, they were God's people, a chosen nation. But not a righteously appointed political state, a moral government. It may be subtle, but there is a difference.

Jesus' early followers, most of whom were Jews, knew that their teacher's message was political—the coming of the kingdom. But not until after his death did they begin to understand that the kingdom was found in the person of Jesus Christ. God's reign was not associated with a single piece of real estate. Instead, God's reign comprised a people whose way of life was shaped by practices of hospitality and love that challenged the prevailing social order. The earliest Christians knew that God's kingdom was visible only to those who "had the eyes to see" it—and once you did see, it became nearly impossible to live any other way.

All that changed when, in the early fourth century, Emperor Constantine did two unthinkable things: he seized power in Christ's name and legalized the Christian faith.

Unlike some Roman emperors, Constantine was politically and militarily challenged for the throne by others with equal standing and claim. In a dream, God directed Constantine to conquer in the sign of Christ (the Greek letters, *chi* and *rho,* that form a cross) and to place that mark on the shields of the army. According to pious legend, Constantine obeyed God. With the cross as its ensign, his army routed the enemy at Milvian Bridge and marched victoriously on to Rome.

Whether the legend is true or not, the story reveals a dramatic change in Christian self-understanding. For four centuries, Christianity was the faith of the martyrs, those whom soldiers murdered. No serious Christian would dream of joining an army. Early Christian literature regularly recounts saints who disobeyed parents and authorities and forswore military service in favor of monastic life. Constantine's dream reversed the usual tale: Jesus Christ bears the sword instead of being beaten down by it.

Instead of being slain like a martyr, Constantine won the battle. In recognition of the Christian God's mercy and power, the new emperor legalized the once-traitorous religion. Christians, weary of vicious persecution under the emperor's ten predecessors, hailed Constantine as the thirteenth apostle, the one able to do what Peter and Paul failed to do: Christianize Rome. As the late historian Roland Bainton would write, the swords of the imperial guard were drawn "no longer to punish but to honor the Christians."[11]

In the wake of legalization, the leaders of church and empire formed new alliances. "After Constantine's edict," states historian David Chidester, "they began to redefine the position of Christianity in the empire as both a religious and a political force. They forged a merger of church and state in which Christianity eventually displaced pagan tradition as the established religion of the Roman Empire. In the process, the Roman Empire became a Christian empire."[12] The Christian religion merged with imperial politics. According to the early Christian historian Eusebius, God had honored his promise to the ancient Jews by establishing a political kingdom of God under Constantine.

The Christian empire delivered peace. But it was peace at a price. Christians had to assent to particular statements of belief or face state charges of heresy; Christians had to join the army; Christians had to wage war against barbarians, the infidels, heretics, and the unbaptized; Christians had to support imperial policy; Christians had to pray for the emperor; Christians had to tithe to the state to maintain the bishops, clergy, and sacred places. Christianity and good citizenship became firmly intertwined.

When I teach church history, I ask students what they think about Constantine. Many think that Christian empire was a good idea—certainly preferable to the alternative of persecution and martyrdom. Others think Christianity would not have survived without legalization or that it would have survived as a much different religion than it is today. Still others think that Constantine's action undermined the genius of early Christianity and turned the faith into a function of imperial power—a position not unlike some devout believers in the fourth century! Occasionally, a class actually gets into an argument over Constantine and Christianity. Even today, people have strong feelings about Christian empire. Being an Episcopalian, a person who has mostly benefited from imperial faith and its European continuation as Christendom, I used to think Constantine a blessing. Now, however, I think writer Verna Dozier may be right: Emperor Constantine's edict constituted "the third fall" of humanity—the first being the fall of Adam and Eve; the second being Israel's demand for a king—whose effect "was to make accommodation [to the kingdom of this world] the mode of the people of God."[13]

ROME IN AMERICA

Although it is difficult to discern the personal religious faith of America's founding fathers, it is not difficult to discern how these men of the Enlightenment felt about Rome. They were enamored of the ancient world, especially a "highly selected" and romanticized vision of republican Rome, a society that embodied "simplicity, patriotism, integrity, a love of justice and of liberty."[14]

The founders were more wary of imperial Rome—as they were of imperial England—but their criticisms typically focused on the corrupted imperial practices rather than on the political idea of empire. If Rome had only maintained the correct balance of power and liberty, of sovereign and subject, the empire might have stood. From Plutarch and Livy to Cicero and Tacitus, classical ideas nurtured the early American imagination as much as biblical ones—God's kingdom and ancient Rome intermixed in the search for national identity.

For people schooled in classics and the Bible, Christian empire proved an easy ideal for national destiny. By the late nineteenth century, the symbols of Christian empire were commonplace. As historian Richard Hughes Seager recounts:

> On 1 May 1893, 200,000 people gathered on the shores of Lake Michigan on Chicago's south side to attend the opening ceremonies of the World's Columbian Exposition, America's quadricentennial salute to Christopher Columbus. Standing beneath a giant Stars and Stripes, President Grover Cleveland pressed a telegraph key that set the Exposition's machinery in motion. While Chicago's 5,000 voice Apollo Choir sang Handel's "Hallelujah Chorus," . . . jets of water streamed from electric fountains; drapery fell from a colossal gilded statue of the Goddess of Liberty. These symbols—the flag, the Goddess of Liberty, and the "Hallelujah Chorus" form the foundation of a myth of America.

As Seager says, these "patriotic, classical, and Christian signs" are the "mythic building blocks" of the "United States [as] both the new imperium and a New Jerusalem, the City of God and man."[15]

Until September 11, 2001, many Americans—mostly those of us born after World War II—thought the Christian imperialism of the World's Columbian Exposition a quaint relic of our grandparents' day. But quietly, deep beneath the language of pluralism and equality, those symbols and sentiments of American Christian imperialism still shape our national culture. The new national security strategy expressed the old ideals that America was both mighty empire and bearer of true faith.

Essayist and poet Wendell Berry pointed out that an epigraph of the security document quotes President Bush's sermon from the National Cathedral on September 14, 2001: "But our responsibility to history is already clear: to answer these attacks and rid the world of evil."[16] Berry then comments, "A government, committing its nation to rid the world of evil, is assuming necessarily that it and its nation are good."[17] And any such government is not just making political claims. It is making theological and moral claims. *What happens,* I wondered, *to those whom this righteous empire deems heretical, evil, or infidels?* Preemptive military action, I guess. "If you are not with us," warned the president repeatedly in speeches after September 11, "you are against us." This attitude resembles that of the Roman Catholic Church when it ruled over European Christendom, an attitude that easily—and sadly—resulted in Crusades, witch hunts, and inquisitions, the worst episodes of all of Christian history.

Even if Christendom is only a vague European memory, the Unites States suffers from a sort of Constantinian hangover. The effects of Emperor Constantine on faith and state just won't go away. Nor will the problems he created when he conflated the City of God and the City of Man. As contemporary theologian Stanley Hauerwas explains Augustine's view of empire: "The earthly city knows not God and is thus characterized by order secured only through violence."[18] Empires always rule by the sword. Is anything else possible?

Even Augustine would say no. Christian empire is an oxymoron, fundamentally an earthly impossibility, despite what may seem to be manifestations of it.

Here outside of Washington, D.C., I live in the ruling metropolis of global empire. I do not find this comforting. As Richard Horsley points out, "Many Americans cannot avoid the awkward feeling that they are now more analogous to imperial Rome than they are to the ancient Middle Eastern people who celebrated their origins in God's liberation . . . and lived in covenantal principles of justice."[19]

Yes, I was and am uneasy. How does a Christian live in empire? Especially when that empire claims, in some way, the blessing of the Christian God? God's reign of peace, a kingdom of love, where swords are beaten into plowshares? What of Jesus' words "The time is fulfilled, and the kingdom of God has come near" (Mark 1:14)? Were such promises a cruel joke, a scriptural taunt of what never will be? How to live *in* the empire and not be *of* it? I have been forced to come to terms with Stanley Hauerwas's assertion, "How to understand the relation between the two cities [is] the central issue for the development of what comes to be called Christian social ethics."[20]

When the president thinks of Christian social ethics, however, I feel fairly confident that no one at the White House understands the complex and subtle doctrines of the two cities—and the implications of that tradition for nation building and empire—especially by people who claim to have the biblical God on their side. Given the historical record of empires, I am pretty sure that even compassionate imperialism will not work. And as I theologically contemplate the

96

national security strategy, this new Bush doctrine, I inwardly hear the warning given by the ancient prophet Zephaniah (2:15): "Is this the exultant city that lived secure, that said to itself, 'I am, and there is no one else'? What a desolation it has become, a lair for wild animals! Everyone who passes by it hisses and shakes the fist."

As Christians respond to the reading of Scripture, this is "the Word of the Lord." Such is the biblical fate of unilateral empires.

Homeland Security

*N*o one has to know that I'm scared, I thought as I walked down the aisle at Safeway, *if I just buy one or two gallons of water in case of a terrorist attack. Two gallons seems normal.*

The Office of Homeland Security had just raised the terror-alert level from yellow to orange—putting the nation at the second-highest warning of possible terrorist attack. Government officials advised residents of major cities to stock up on water and batteries—and to have a supply of duct tape and plastic sheeting on hand.

My husband dismissed it all as political fearmongering. I, on the other hand, worried. "Just a few supplies," I told him as I went off to the grocery store.

I reached the section marked Water and looked around. The shelves were completely empty. "Sorry, ma'am," the stock clerk told me. "There's not a bottle of water to be had at any local Safeway. All sold out." The store was also low on nonperishable food like energy bars and cans of tuna. The situation was exactly the same at

Home Depot. Shelves stripped of duct tape and plastic sheeting. Empty. My Homeland Security–inspired shopping trip would have been a complete failure if not for the few D batteries I found at the variety store around the corner from my house. In case of biological terrorism, at least our flashlights would work.

Homeland security. Until very recently, those words were not about politics, they were about faith. In the phrase, I inwardly heard the longing echoes of "Land of Rest," a traditional American folk hymn:

Jerusalem, my happy home,
When shall I come to thee?
When shall my sorrows have an end?
Thy joys when shall I see?[1]

As a Christian, I trust that I have a homeland, one that is secure in God's care. But that homeland is not a political nation. I am only a sojourner, an alien citizen of the United States; by virtue of my baptism in Christian faith, my primary citizenship is in God's city. Throughout church history, Christians in many nations have tried to associate their geography with God's holy city (for example, the Byzantine Empire, the medieval Holy Roman Empire, or the realm of Russian tsars), but such biblical territorial claims have always resulted in some tragic corruption of the Christian gospel. The homeland of Jesus' followers is God's city, a non-geographical city embodied in the way of life of its people in the present—and a city whose full revelation awaits some future time. The city is, as much of Christian theology has affirmed, "already and not yet." Today, some people identify the biblical homeland as the state of Israel or the United States of America. But neither can truly claim that title. The homeland of God's faithful remains a promise, both a way of life and a place of rest for which God's people still long.

I do hope for a land of rest, as described in the traditional American hymn, a peaceful homeland. This is a holy hope, the same hope expressed by biblical patriarchs and prophets. The Scriptures and Christian tradition teach that the hope for a homeland is theologically fulfilled in the person of Jesus Christ. And that one day the long awaited city will be more clearly manifest in creation. In the meanwhile, however, God's people are promised neither an earthly homeland nor security. I am not convinced that a government department can deliver either—when God's people have been waiting since the time of Abraham for both. To seek homeland security is, at best, a misguided quest.

HOMELAND

When I was a girl, my agnostic grandfather used to criticize religion that "was no earthly good" and ridicule "pie-in-the-sky" faith. He grew up as a Methodist evangelical, and his understanding of Christianity had been shaped by sentimental, even escapist, revivalist songs with lyrics like "This world is not my home; I'm just a-passing through." In my grandfather's view, Christianity was more concerned with heavenly mansions than it was with improving life on earth—a scathing criticism from a working-class machinist who struggled to keep a roof over his family's head during the Great

Depression. Church, he had come to believe, was a spiritual salve for the hopeless poor and for rich hypocrites. Eventually he rejected the church in favor of armchair Marxism. He was certainly a spiritual freethinker. To him, religion was the opiate of the people, and he wanted no part of it.

Like my grandfather, I grew up around fervent evangelical religion. But so much had changed from the days in which he ridiculed "Holy Rollers." The Christians I knew barely spoke of life after death or the gold-lined streets of heaven. Indeed, they were a fairly worldly group who drove expensive cars to church, lived in nice houses, sent their children to private schools, traveled around the world (often under the guise of missionary trips), drank beer and wine (sometimes on the sly), and went to R-rated movies.

Although evangelical Christians I grew up with used different words to describe their faith ("I've been born again") than did culturally accommodating Presbyterians and Episcopalians, by the 1980s, their lives (although not their theology) resembled those of their liberal Protestant kin. When they sang "This world is not my home, I'm just a-passing through. . . . My pleasure and my hopes are placed beyond the blue," they did not sound as if they really meant it. By the final decades of the twentieth century, most American Christians appeared comfortable with the idea of a blessed earthly homeland in addition to a heavenly one. In the early 1990s, one evangelical organization nicely captured this turn of events by publishing a book called *No Longer Exiles*.[2] Although evangelical Protestants often spoke in a language of cultural alienation and found the terminology of "culture wars" politically expedient, even they discovered that home was a pretty nice place. American Protestantism, like American religion in general, has been tamed by American culture. As writer Alan Wolfe says, "We are all mainstream now."[3]

New Testament writers, however, seem ambivalent about the whole idea of a homeland. To describe it, which they rarely did, they used the Greek term, *patris,* the root for the English word *patriotic,* which refers to one's fatherland or one's own native place.

The most significant homeland story in the Gospels appears in Luke 4:18, where Jesus returns to his hometown of Nazareth and preaches: "The Spirit of the Lord is upon me, because he has anointed me to bring good news to the poor." His fellow townspeople rejected his claim, leading Jesus to conclude, "No prophet is accepted in the prophet's hometown" (Luke 4:24). This criticism did not go over well with his neighbors. They responded by driving him out of town and trying to hurl him off a cliff. For Jesus, his earthly homeland was a dangerous place for someone choosing to do God's work. Indeed, in Hebrews 11:13–16, the writer describes those living the life of faith as people who "were strangers and foreigners on the earth," men and women who were "seeking a homeland . . . a better country, a heavenly one." Or according to Philippians 3:20, "our commonwealth is in heaven."

Although some Christians have used these ideas to justi-fy antiworldliness or withdrawal from society, the funda-mental truth remains: the homeland of God's people is not a theocratic earthly nation. God's real estate is, theologian

Barry Harvey writes, the "confession of Christ's Lordship—celebrated in its Eucharistic gatherings and lived out daily in a holy life of service and fellowship."[4]

Occasionally, as was the case for medieval Catholics and nineteenth-century mainline Protestants, Christians have rejected the otherworldly orientation of God's realm by making the kingdom of God coterminous with human society. In both cases, the body politic—or the hoped-for body politic—is identified as God's political order. Medieval popes believed they ruled over the earth in Christ's stead, and earnest American Protestants thought they were bringing God's city to earth through prayer and democratic politics. Throughout history, identifying one's homeland as God's formed the basis for Christendom, the earthly reign of the church. The confusion started with the Emperor Constantine in 313 CE and, in Europe and America, continued well into our times. The most recent manifestation of the tendency is the political objective of some evangelical Protestants to reclaim, redeem, or retake America as a Christian nation.[5]

Historically, the United States proved uniquely poised to interpret itself as God's homeland, a kind of New World Israel, given to European Christians by God as a second chance at Eden. Our forebears busily refashioned Christian tradition to American ideals of freedom, democracy, liberty, and capitalism. But there was a price to be paid for that accommodation. For most American Christians, pulling apart the interwoven threads of "Christian" and "American" has proved difficult. Indeed, the relationship between faith and nation has been so confusing that, in the minds of many, despite the separation of church and state, America is a

Christian nation. There may be no established national church, but God himself guides, blesses, and oversees the American experiment, "the last great hope of earth." In America, the government may not start or sponsor a church, but the nation itself is an embodiment of the will and plan of the biblical God.

In recent years, as evangelical Protestants articulated a political theology of American Christian nationhood, some mainline Protestant theologians have begun to recover the idea of God's heavenly reign and reject the cozy worldliness that had been the hallmark of their denominations. In an ironic reversal, mainline Protestant theology (not the evangelical Protestant who did so in the last century) now tends to emphasize Scripture's exile tradition, "that the church exists today as resident aliens, an adventurous colony in a society of unbelief."[6] They have returned to the biblical idea of the church as Abraham's children, strangers and foreigners whose commonwealth is in heaven.

That Christians are an exile people seems an apt—and even providential—reminder in light of so-called homeland security. The Christian *patris* is a distant realm, and our loyalty to any secular homeland is that of an exile community. We work, have children, raise families, care for the poor, work for the betterment of our communities, pay taxes. We try to figure out what Jesus meant when he said, "Render to Caesar the things that are Caesar's and to God, the things that are God's" (Mark 12:17). That is harder than it seems. Christians believe, like Jews, that as the Psalmist says, "the earth is the Lord's and all that is therein" (Ps. 24:1). Thus at the heart of Christian citizenship is a dilemma: Christians submit to Caesar so long as Caesar's laws do not conflict with the Lordship of Jesus Christ. Christian patriotism is practicing a way of life based in the virtues of faith, hope, and love. We are citizens, only secondarily, of our earthly homelands. As Christians, we may or may not appreciate the ideals, politics, or policies of the country in which we reside.

That means, of course, that there are no easy answers when it comes to issues of Christian citizenship. Christians must consider every political issue theologically in light of the tradition, authority, practice, and wisdom of the faith community, with a keen sense of their primary status as alien citizens. Faith is a kind of risk culture, lending itself to what theologian Barry Harvey calls "holy insecurity," as the citizens of God's city "must always struggle to detect the delicate counterpoint of the Spirit" to mediate between engaging the world and challenging it.[7]

SECURITY

If holy insecurity is foundational to life in God's city, the quest for earthly security is theologically at odds with the teaching of both the Hebrew and Christian Scriptures. As Jesus discovered when his neighbors tried to throw him off a cliff, and as scores of biblical prophets had found out before him, God promises no earthly security to those who believe and follow.

The word for *security* in the New Testament is *asphalizo,* "making secure." Evidently, early Christians were so unconcerned with security that the word is used only four times in their stories about Jesus. Three of those usages refer to the seal on Jesus' tomb being made secure—so that no one could steal his body. And the fourth use tells of the apostles being thrown into prison and being made secure in the stocks. In the Gospels and the Book of Acts, security is something that Roman soldiers do. And it appears that it is something done to Christians to keep them in their place.

What is security? *Security* is, in essence, being powerful or rich enough to create (at least) an illusion of being safe from danger, of controlling events, people, and situations so that we are not exposed to loss or risk. We tend to think of security as freedom from evil, war, and crime. When we are secure, we can depend on the future and our own means to get there. Rich Americans are experts at security—the middle and upper classes cushion existence with everything from gated communities to financial securities. Indeed, the American tie between money and security is so close that, on the eve of the Great Depression, the prominent African American minister Howard Thurman identified possessions as idols of security. He reminded clergy of an essential task of ministry: "We must refuse to be caught in the present demand for things and must find our security in the reality of God and the spiritual tasks to which He has set our hands."[8]

The terrorist attack on New York, America's financial center, killed more than human beings. It destroyed the illusion of American safety—a security built on international trade, bank accounts, and stock portfolios. We believed we were protected by our separate continent and too rich and powerful to be hurt by fundamentalist violence—unlike poor countries in other parts of the world, where such attacks are tragically common.

The hole in the New York skyline was, to borrow a theological image used by Dorothee Soelle before September 11, "a window of vulnerability." Not the kind of window of which a military planner speaks—the place where an enemy might attack. But as Soelle pointed out, "Every window makes us vulnerable and is a sign of relationship, receptivity, communication," and "the window of vulnerability is a window toward heaven."[9] She goes on to argue that vulnerability opens the way to true peace. And sadly, human beings often confuse peace with security. Security is a closing of the window, something we "increasingly neuroticize," for "our need for it becomes insatiable; one can never be secure enough."[10]

The attacks on that late summer day opened a theological window for Americans: to recognize that security is a false idol. We were the victims of violence. I think the rest of the world sympathized with us because, stripped of our superpower status, we were suddenly vulnerable to the violence and suffering that afflicts the whole globe—and to which we are often blind. And that was a gift of grace: to see that human security is flimsy at best, while the deepest security is found in the love of God through the vulnerability of Jesus' cross. Biblical tradition witnesses to the illusion of earthly security: from Pharaoh's army drowning in the Red Sea to the apostles in chains in Roman jails, the Word teaches the folly of trusting in possessions and power to keep us safe from harm. Faith is not about security; rather it is about certainty in God's love—no matter what.

Throughout biblical history, instead of making themselves secure, God's faithful people, like Abraham, left homeland and security seeking "the city . . . whose architect and builder is God" (Heb. 11:10). They did not look for security on earth—and certainly few of them found it. According to the writer of Hebrews:

> Others were tortured, refusing to accept release, in order to obtain a better resurrection. Others suffered mocking and flogging, and even chains and imprisonment. They were stoned to death, they were sawn in two, they were killed by the sword; they went about in skins of sheep and goats, destitute, persecuted, tormented—of whom the world was not worthy. They wandered in deserts and mountains, and in caves and holes in the ground [Heb. 11:36–38].

In biblical narratives, earthly security is illusory, whereas God's security is both trustworthy and unpredictable. Like the Holy Spirit, the Wind of God moves where it will, breathing life into all creation. The security offered by God is an adventure worth living because it empowers us to live in the true freedom and liberty of God's love and justice. At times, God's people do live peaceably: under wise judges, when David was king, during Solomon's reign. We are to welcome and celebrate when it happens, but we also must recognize that it does not happen often in human history. And Abraham remains the exemplar of faith—"he set out, not knowing where he was going" (Heb. 11:8). Even his greatest act of faith, his willingness to murder his son Isaac out of obedience to God, remains a chilling witness to the fundamental *insecurity* of faith.

The other sobering reminder of faith's insecurity is the cross of Jesus Christ. Following God in faith, doing God's work without wavering, Jesus was killed because his allegiance to God's realm challenged and frightened those in his homeland. From the baptism of Jesus and his temptation in the wilderness, the Christian tradition teaches that faith leads to the insecurity modeled in the crucifixion and resurrection—not to the earthly security of *patris*. The only homeland security is found when God is our security. In his paraphrase of Psalm 90, eighteenth-century hymn writer Isaac Watts wrote:

> O God, our help in ages past,
> Our hope for years to come,
> Our shelter from the stormy blast,
> And our eternal home.
> Under the shadow of thy throne,
> Thy saints have dwelt secure;
> Sufficient is thine arm alone,
> And our defense is sure.[11]

The cross is our *patris;* God's peace is our security. The goal of God's people is *shalom,* dedication to a way of life that embodies peace—not security. Ours is a spirituality of exile, of quest for a homeland that remains elusive, and of trust that God's love is our only true security.

THE HOUSEHOLD OF *SHALOM*

Whereas physical security is the exclusive possession of the rich, Old Testament scholar Walter Brueggemann reminds us that "*shalom* is never the private property of the few."[12] The Scriptures envision a secure world, but its security is founded on *shalom*. As Brueggemann summarizes the biblical narrative:

> The central vision of world history in the Bible is that all of creation is one, every creature in community with every other, living in harmony and security toward the joy and well-being of every other creature. . . . The most staggering expression of the vision is that *all persons* are *children of a single family,* members of a single tribe, heirs of a single hope, and bearers of a single destiny, namely, the care and management of all God's creation.[13]

In addition to *patris,* another Greek word in the New Testament, *oikos,* sometimes translated as "household" or "home." Unlike *patris,* "homeland," New Testament writers extol *oikos*—God's household—as Brueggemann defines it: "that all persons are children of a single family, members of a single tribe, heirs of a single hope, and bearers of a single destiny."[14] That is *oikos.*

Much of the New Testament can be read as people switching their loyalty from *patris* to *oikos.* As the Apostle Paul reminded the Ephesians, Christ's followers were no longer Jews or Greeks, Roman citizens or slaves, male or female; they became part of a single household, God's home. In doing so, they placed themselves in jeopardy—willing to risk the security of their social status and privilege in favor of embodying God's *shalom.* The Romans understood the threat posed as people rejected loyalty to the homeland for the peace of God's household. They deemed Christians as traitors, a threat to the state, and they willingly persecuted and tortured the *oikos.*

The Christian tradition never grants those who follow God either an earthly homeland or physical security. Instead, it promises that all people will, in the power of the cross, be brought into God's household and gifted with God's peace and God's well-being. Brueggemann underscores its reality:

> It is well-being that exists in the very midst of threats—from sword and drought and wild animals. It is well-being of a material, physical, historical kind, not idyllic "pie-in-the-sky" but "salvation" in the midst of trees and crops and enemies—in the very places where people always have to cope with anxiety, to struggle for survival, and to deal with temptation. . . . *Shalom* comes only to the inclusive, embracing community that excludes none.[15]

Homeland security? Maybe. Maybe not. Holy insecurity? Absolutely. For biblical people, only God's *oikos* of *shalom* is a guarantee, the vision of which draws closer as we passionately pursue its way of life, the peace of God's own city. It is a longing hope, a certain hope that may be realized even in a time of terrorism, division, and fear.

7

Peace and the City

By the summer of 2002, I wondered whether Christ Church could ever comprehend my anxieties about the two cities, about Christian ethics, and about practicing faith as a way of life. Just shy of the first September 11 anniversary, I resigned from my position there. Ostensibly, I chose to do so because of budget cuts. I knew, however, that was not the whole reason. I ached spiritually. I needed to be part of a community that understood the difference between the City of God and the City of Man. Although a number of individuals in the congregation tried to see clearly, Christ Church's history blurred the boundaries too much.

For me, the final straw was the main Sunday service on July 7, celebrating Independence Day. Following patriotic readings (in lieu of a sermon), the congregation sang the national anthem more vigorously than they had ever sung any Christian hymn. I stood outside at the windows and listened. When they finished the second verse, "Then conquer we must, when our cause it is just. . . . And the star-spangled banner in triumph shall wave o'er the land of the free and the home of the brave," the minister declared: "Go in peace to love and serve the Lord." Apparently, no one noticed the irony as they jubilantly shouted back: "Thanks be to God!"

Although all of this was done under the rubric of pastoral care and to offer people familiar comforts, my family needed *church*—not the form of chapel religion embodied so powerfully by Christ Church. My husband, whose tolerance for civil religion is even lower than mine, had stopped attending Christ Church months earlier. Richard had discovered an interesting congregation across the river in the heart of Washington, D.C. Just three blocks from the White House, the Church of the Epiphany was founded in 1842 as a city mission. Epiphany claimed a glorious past as a downtown pillar congregation, whose roster of distinguished Americans included bishops, senators, ambassadors, and cabinet members. Richard liked it. And there was no flag hanging in the sanctuary.

In late summer, I told the clergy staff I would be leaving Christ Church. On the first Sunday I worshiped at Epiphany, I looked around and cried. Epiphany's building is shabby, and its congregation is small. It is not prestigious anymore. Since the 1960s—and like many mainline urban congregations—the church had suffered a decline of membership, influence, and wealth.

I was not weepy, however, over some glorious lost past. Things were changing at Epiphany. For about a decade, the church had been slowly rediscovering a sense of identity and vocation. Although small, the congregation was surprisingly diverse—white and black and brown, mixed classes, young and old, gay and straight, people of different backgrounds and education, those who live in houses and those who live on the streets. I thought of Garrison Keillor's description of a very similar congregation in New York, "A real good anthology of faith. I felt glad to be there."[1] I too felt glad to be there. To me, the diversity reflected the kingdom of heaven: "saints from every tribe and language and people and nation" (Rev. 5:9).

I knew these people opened their doors to the homeless, fed more than two hundred people every Sunday morning, participated in numerous social justice ministries in Washington, housed a growing ministry of healing prayer and labyrinth walking, and offered exquisite music to the community. My intuition told me that these people knew something about God's city and about being a different kind of church.

I wanted to be part of Epiphany, but I was afraid. Deep under the church is Metro Center, the hub of Washington's subway system. Three blocks away sits the White House. The church is surrounded by government offices and the media. Epiphany, like St. Paul's Chapel in New York City, stands near one of the intended targets of September 11. Just driving to church, past the concrete barriers and newly installed security measures, reminded me that the threats continued. Would I endanger my family every week to worship God? What if there were a gas attack? A car bomb? What if? What if?

I prayed. I started to realize how much fear had shaped my life over the past year. What better place to be than in a church if terrorists struck again? For some reason, God seemed to be calling us to the heart of this American darkness, to witness to the power of Christ's kingdom. Could I find peace in the city?

MOVING THE FURNITURE

Christians talk about peace. Christians believe in peace. But it has been very clear in the past couple of years how hard it is to practice peace as a way of life. Leaving Christ Church, I reflected on the ways in which congregational history shapes contemporary practice—including the practice of peacemaking. Many people at Christ Church cared about peace, but the church's history prevented them from embracing or practicing it in ways that would challenge received military or political options.

Christ Church's memorials celebrate George Washington and Robert E. Lee—both military generals. In addition to two huge memorial tablets, the church further enshrined their memory by marking their pews with engraved silver plaques. The AAA tour book of Alexandria extols Christ Church, saying "the inside remains pristine and almost untouched since its early days." Indeed, Christ Church carefully preserves its past.

Other than Washington and Lee, however, no prominent memorials celebrate other parishioners. The chancel is framed with an American flag and an Episcopal one—the whole thing conveys the impression of a romanticized, aristocratic Virginia version of God and country. Months before I left, I realized that it would be difficult for many of the

Christ Church congregants to either wrestle with or understand the complex tensions between the City of God and the
City of Man—especially when surrounded by symbols honoring war, when the church building itself reinforces the state
and its power. There was too much historical and social pres-
sure against even raising the issue.

Like the more socially prestigious Christ Church in
Alexandria, Epiphany has a history of church and state as
well. And it has a plaque on a historic pew. Epiphany's
memorial commemorates a politician: Jefferson Davis, sena-
tor from Mississippi and president of the Confederacy. Davis
attended Epiphany in the 1850s, as the crisis over American
slavery deepened. He, of course, staunchly defended the
practice of slaveholding.

Some Washington residents took note of Davis's church
membership and believed his views at odds with the gospel.
One, Edwin Stanton, who later served in President Lincoln's
cabinet, complained to Epiphany's minister that Davis's position on slavery was inconsistent with the gospel. The minister, himself from South Carolina, called on Mr. Stanton and
defended Epiphany's inclusiveness as a church that preached
Christ and the gospel—from there, the political chips could
fall where they might. Stanton, impressed by the minister's
position, joined the church.

Davis's pew, however, was destined to become a piece of
contested real estate. Eventually, Davis left Washington—and
Epiphany—for Richmond, Virginia. Stanton, who later urged
Lincoln to free the slaves, moved into Davis's family pew.

After the Civil War, the Daughters of the Confederacy
reclaimed the pew for the Southern cause, placing a brass

plaque on it honoring Jefferson Davis. Shortly thereafter, the plaque was stolen by, it was suspected, an African American member of the congregation unhappy with Davis's glorification. The plaque, however, was eventually returned and replaced. For many years thereafter, the Daughters of the Confederacy decorated it with flowers on Memorial Day and Confederate Veterans' Day. The plaque remains on the pew to this day.

By the midtwentieth century, however, the Davis pew became a source of ironic discomfort for an increasingly diverse congregation. Although the congregation always comprised those of all political persuasions, it supported the Civil Rights and the peace movements. As civil unrest roiled its downtown neighborhood, Epiphany fed and sheltered protesters and marchers. As surrounding structures burned in riots, African American activists protected the church from unruly mobs. The congregation had become known as a place of peace, a haven for those defending the rights of the poor and oppressed.

Sometime in the midtwentieth century (no one knows exactly when), someone (no one remembers who) moved the Jefferson Davis pew from the main sanctuary to a side chapel. The Daughters of the Confederacy stopped coming. The plaque is still there, but you have to search for it. Epiphany had learned that a congregation may need to live with history, but that history need not determine the future. You might remember a champion of slavery was once a member of your church, but you can gently sideline his legacy.

Nobody talks of Jefferson Davis anymore. Memorials in the church building honor a host of Epiphany saints past—the famous and those remembered only by God. We talk about homelessness, racism, justice, and peacemaking. About a good worship service, hard weeks, illness and childbirth, Sunday school, and the cake served at coffee hour. Epiphany is not a perfect place, but the congregation is trying to deal honestly with its own history and create a truly multicultural Christian community. *Maybe,* I thought, after belonging to Epiphany for a few months, *history does not have to repeat itself.* Epiphany taught me that if you are willing to move the furniture, you might just change the future. At Christ Church, no one would move the furniture. For generations, people kept coming—and are still coming—who like the way their spiritual room is arranged. But Epiphany is willing to change. And sometimes if you just move the furniture, you can better see the City of God.

CHURCH AS *HOSPITIUM*

From what I have learned about Epiphany, the greatest thing that ever happened in the congregation's history is that the sanctuary served as a hospital during the Civil War. In the pews where we now sit, doctors and nurses healed the sick and comforted the dying. When soldiers have died in your pews, it is hard to glorify war. You know its costs. Epiphany did not simply honor the war dead, it allowed their blood to splatter its floors and walls. In stark contrast to Christ Church, Epiphany is neither pristine nor untouched.

The English word *hospital* comes from the Latin *hospitium,* meaning "the relations between host and guest; the welcoming, reception, or accommodation of guests." *Hospi-*

tium is the root word of several related English words: *hospital, hospice, hostel, host,* and *hospitality.* The *Oxford Latin
Dictionary* specifically defines it as "an establishment that
provides rest for travelers."

More than a century after the Civil War, Epiphany is still
a *hospitium* in all of its Latin senses—a place of respite for
pilgrims, a place of caring for others, a place of healing, a
place of welcome. Two interconnected Christian practices—
healing and hospitality—frame its daily life. And it welcomes
all who come through its doors—offering, in particular, hospitality to the homeless and hungry. These twin practices
strengthen the congregation's ability to embody God's reign
and its virtues. We do not do that perfectly, of course, but
we do understand that we are pilgrims seeking that City
of God.

Epiphany has practiced healing for a long time—from its
early days as a city mission through the medical practices of
the Civil War doctors and nurses to the ministry of pastoral
care exercised by its people and clergy. In recent years, the
congregation added a rite of healing prayer to the regular
Sunday service. Every week, following the Eucharist, the
majority of parishioners move directly from receiving the
bread and wine to a small prayer chapel. There, a healing
minister prays and marks each person with the sign of the
cross: "Come, Holy Spirit, and with the laying on of hands
and the anointing with oil in the name of Jesus Christ, fill this
your faithful servant with the healing power of your love."
For the people of Epiphany, this prayer has become a natural practice—a personal empowerment that confirms God's
presence in our lives.

It takes, I think, humility to request healing prayer—to admit that something is out of one's control, that an illness or problem or fear cannot be handled alone. The ministry of healing recognizes that wholeness grows in the mealy soil of human brokenness, when we allow God's spirit to sow grace. Healing prayer is a sort of pilgrimage into fundamental truths about the limits of the human condition and surrender to God's love, a ritual that embodies the whole message of the gospel in the simple acts of prayer, laying on of hands, and marking with a cross.

At Epiphany, I have experienced healing from my fears. I have been able, finally, to enter into the universe shaped by the Eucharist and worship, unencumbered by the symbols of the state. Until being there a few months, I did not realize how much my soul ached with fear, anger, bitterness, anxiety, worry, dread, sadness, stress, and confusion. There are many ways that September 11 broke me. I was not broken in the sense of being destroyed. But I certainly experienced a sense of my own vulnerability. A well-hidden fear of my own fragility and mortality surfaced, as has a sense of the world's brokenness. A deep grief gripped me. How far humanity is from God's dream of peace! I think Epiphany has taught me about the holy insecurity of faith, the kind of insecurity theologian Dorothee Soelle described as the "window of vulnerability" that allows us to see God's city.[2] Every week, I continue to seek healing myself as I live in a city where the window of vulnerability is still wide open, beseeching God for wisdom to live wisely and without fear. Asking God to heal me, my nation, and the world through the power of love.

I think the terrorist attacks, the continued fears of terrorism, and the wars in the Middle East broke many people. But many have not been able to admit it. Perhaps they have been too embarrassed or ashamed to say they are afraid. Perhaps we have no words to name it. Epiphany has taught me that there is no shame in brokenness and the sense of vulnerability that comes from holy insecurity. It has enabled me to realize how close those who are wounded live to the heart of God. Indeed, recognizing our vulnerability and giving up illusions of control may be fundamental to authentic Christian spirituality in post–September 11 America.

Something strange happens when people recognize vulnerability and brokenness. They open their doors and let others in. Indeed, the Latin word for host, *hospes,* also means guest or stranger. In the mysterious economy of the City of God, the healed become hosts; convalescents offer care; the weary provide places of rest. As we see God in our own suffering, we learn to see God in the suffering of others. Healing is not a private practice. Rather, healing and hospitality are intimately related: Soelle's window of vulnerability leads to openness in community.

Not long ago, I preached on a Sunday morning at Epiphany. I arrived early—before the end of the eight o'clock service, the service geared toward the homeless. As I walked into the church, a woman was talking loudly to her invisible friend; several men were sleeping on back pews; and some people were standing and singing a hymn. About two hundred people were at that Eucharist—they were an amazing cross section of humanity for a church! It was unruly, disorderly, and utterly hospitable. And *holy.* Indeed, a church member, who first came to the church when she was home-less, once commented to me, "Epiphany is the first church I ever visited that treated me like a human being. Nobody looked at me as if I was going to steal something." I thought of Jesus' words from the Gospel of Matthew (25:35), "I was a stranger and you welcomed me."

In her book *Making Room: Recovering Hospitality as a Christian Tradition,* theologian Christine Pohl argues that "hospitality is a way of life fundamental to Christian identi-ty."[3] At Epiphany, I have begun to understand the transfor-mative power of belonging to a community with hospitality as its heart. As Pohl says:

> Although we often think of hospitality as a tame and pleasant practice, Christian hospitality has always had a subversive, coun-tercultural dimension. "Hospitality is resistance," as one person from the Catholic Worker observed. Especially when the larger society disregards or dishonors certain persons, small acts of respect and welcome are potent far beyond themselves.

Indeed, she argues that "some of the most complex political and ethical tensions center around recognizing or treating people as equals. . . . For much of church history, Christians addressed concerns about recognition and human dignity within their practices of hospitality."[4]

Pohl wrote several years ago, but her discussion about hospitality possesses even greater force for Christians strug-gling to understand the mission of God's people in the world we are living in now. As hospitality issues from healing, so healing is the result of hospitality. And not just personal heal-ing. For Christians, the healing of political, ethical, religious, and racial tensions is made possible by the practice of hospitality. Not only are healing and hospitality intimately connected, but hospitality and peacemaking are absolutely linked. For American Christians, the ramifications are startling and, perhaps, painful. If we want to rid the world of terrorism, if we want to be safe, we must welcome our enemies. We must offer shelter to strangers. We must heal by hosting.

All of this has consequences for the ways in which Christians understand church and state—and for the practice of Christian citizenship. Radical hospitality depends on emptying oneself of privilege and control: "When hospitality involves more than entertaining family and friends, when it crosses social boundaries and builds community, when it meets significant human needs and reflects divine generosity, *we often find hosts who see themselves in some way as marginal to the larger society.*"[5]

Christian hospitality involves, as Pohl puts it, "a deliberate withdrawal from prevailing understandings of power, status, and possessions." Good hosts are "distinguished from the larger society by their practices, commitments, and distinctive way of life." In short, the whole tradition of Christian hospitality implies that "hospitality still finds its most effective location on the edges of society, where it is offered by hosts who have a sense of their own alien status."[6]

Christians comfortable with civil religion have no sense of their alien status. Those who conflate church and state can never offer the kind of hospitality that embraces, liberates, and empowers people by embodying God's unbounded love. Only *civitas peregrina,* those who understand the church as *hospitium,* can lead the way of peace.

THE SAN DAMIANO CROSS

Not long after we arrived at Epiphany, the church dedicated a new cross for the healing chapel. The cross is a copy of the San Damiano crucifix, an Italian icon from the twelfth century.

The San Damiano crucifix would be a lovely artifact in most cases, but the cross possesses special significance in Christian history. In the spring of 1206, young Francis of Assisi knelt before the crucifix in the ruins of the Church of San Damiano, praying for guidance in his life: "Most high, glorious God, enlighten the darkness of my heart and give me, Lord, a right faith, a certain hope, a perfect charity. Give me, Lord, wisdom and discernment, so that I may carry out your true and holy will."

As he prayed, he heard a voice say, "Francis, rebuild my church." Francis took the command literally. He took silk from his father's storehouse, sold it, and with the proceeds bought bricks to repair the walls. Brick by brick, he and his friends rebuilt the building. Eventually, he understood that God was not directing him to restore a building. Rather, Francis was called to renew the church as the people of God—to rekindle the purity and vision of the gospel in the church, an institution corrupted by wealth and political power.

Over the last four or five years, Epiphany has come to identify with St. Francis's attempt to renew the church as God's people and rekindle apostolic faith. The congregation's growing sense of vocation echoes God's call to St. Francis, "Rebuild my church." And indeed, brick by brick, the people of Epiphany are struggling, even as Francis did, to live as God's people in the city, to embody Christ's love amid poverty, division, and fear. As the Reverend Randolph Charles, Epiphany's priest, says, "St. Francis was a man of the poor, he cherished creation, and he was a peacemaker. He just fits our parish."

And these days, St. Francis fits in an unexpected way: as a Christian who sought to share faith with Muslims in the midst of war.

As a young man, Francis served as a knight. Wounded in battle, he knew the physical suffering, mental agony, and spiritual pain of war. His recovery led to his conversion from war to peace, from soldier of the state to servant of God's peace. As a friar during the Crusades, Francis became increasingly distressed by the continual warfare between Christians and Muslims. And he became convinced that the Crusades would stop if Muslims understood the love of Christ—a love obscured by violence.

Francis dreamed of making a pilgrimage to Jerusalem "to end the senseless bloodshed between Christians and Muslims."[7] With the holy city as his goal, he envisioned a peace mission to Muslims. After he first attempted to meet with Muslims in Morocco and Spain, Francis and some of his brothers accompanied the Fifth Crusade to Egypt. They hoped to cross into enemy territory and convince Sultan al-Kamil of the peace of the Christian message.

Although some Christians of our time may be uneasy with Francis's desire to convert the sultan, the idea of missionary work among Muslims was radically new and quite liberal. Francis grew up with the idea that the Saracens, or Muslims, were infidels—uncivilized heathens who deserved to die for their rebellion against the Christian God. That Francis would embrace the idea of preaching to Muslims was nothing less than a total conversion from the medieval perspective that infidels should be killed to the idea that God loves all people and wants a relationship with them.

The day after five thousand crusaders were killed in Egypt, Francis and his fellow friar, Illuminato, crossed the battle lines while quoting the New Testament, "I send you out as sheep in the midst of wolves; so be wise as serpents and innocent as doves . . . for men will flog you and drag you before governors and kings for my sake" (Matt. 10:16–18). The two men were arrested by a Saracen patrol and brought before the sultan. He asked Francis if the two were messengers or if they wanted to become Muslims. Francis said they were sent by God to save his soul—and asked for a theological disputation with the sultan's holy men. The sultan granted his request and offered Francis his hospitality.

For days in the desert, the dialogue went on. Francis continued to urge the sultan to convert. Eventually, the sultan said he could not change his beliefs and granted the friars safe passage back to camp. When he returned, Francis convinced the Christians to make a truce. They refused, however, to make peace. In early November, the Christian soldiers laid siege to the Egyptian town of Damietta. In fewer than forty-eight hours, in one of the Crusades' most brutal battles, they killed more than seventy-five thousand of the city's inhabitants. When the hardened crusaders entered the city, the gruesome carnage made even them cry. It took three months to clean up the bodies and debris. Francis stayed and cared for the hungry, the sick, and the dying.

Of these months, biographer Adrian House says that Francis had "undergone a succession of psychological experiences unpleasant enough to crack even a saint." His peace mission failed. "He had also observed," writes House, "that the Muslim al-Kamil had demonstrated a greater humanity and desire for peace than his Christian counterpart."[8] God evidently knew the truth of the matter: the medieval church needed to be rebuilt. Confusing an earthly kingdom with the reign of God, the church of St. Francis's day had lost its soul to riches and power and war. Christians sold their birthright in order to politically control Jerusalem and the Middle East. How painful it must have been for Francis. His heart must have broken.

Hanging above the altar in Epiphany's healing chapel is a copy of the cross that converted St. Francis from a man of war to a man of peace—the San Damiano cross. Every week, I kneel at the rail before it to receive the grace of healing prayer. I need that. My heart still breaks over the pain and suffering of this world.

Looking back over the past two years, I do not think most American churches have handled their role very well—to understand our citizenship in God's city, to live lives of Christian virtue, and to practice peace. I think that we have given in to fear. In fact, most of us wanted to shut the window of vulnerability tight. We have traded certainty in God's city for security in the earthly one. We have been very busy rebuilding the walls of Rome.

Yet through the window that remains open at Epiphany, I find myself once again in the company of St. Francis. I hear his prayer: "Lord, make us servants of your peace." After the healing minister makes the cross on my forehead with oil, I open my eyes and I look around. Others kneel at the rail with me. Behind us, a long line of parishioners stretches into the sanctuary waiting to kneel here, before the San Damiano cross. At Epiphany, there are no American flags, no United We Stand signs. We know our brokenness. We know the brokenness of the world. In a way, everyone at Epiphany is homeless; we are experienced wayfarers in this world. We know healing comes only through God's hospitality. We are guests in God's house, strangers and pilgrims on the streets of Washington. Funny, it has been that way for a long time. During the Civil War, Epiphany was known as a place of peace—Christ's peace—and in wartime Washington the church was suspected of treason because of it. Now, a century and a half later, we are still led by peace.

Most of the time, I am in the City of Man, three blocks from the throne of American empire—so close that I can almost touch the powers and principalities of this world. On my knees at the San Damiano cross, I am in the City of God, a city populated by the *civitas peregrina*. Healed by the power of love. Hosts, guests, strangers, friends. We are all bricklayers, really. God's people rebuilding the church. *Bricklayers of the City of God.*

Epiphany is not the perfect church. Not everyone understands the difference between the two cities. Every week, one congregant who wears a large God Bless America button on his lapel tries to turn the prayers of the people into a prowar bully pulpit. I have begun to think that God has put him there to remind us that the City of Man and the City of God still intertwine in this fallen world. Every time he prays, no matter that I struggle to pray his prayers, he reminds me that I hold dual citizenship. That I am both a Christian and an American. That is not an easy thing these days.

Most of Epiphany's people intuit that their primary identity is, however, that of citizenship in God's realm. However we navigate the tensions between the two cities, Washington will always be our lesser love. I am glad to be in church. I feel welcome in this Christian community, as in the words of the Isaac Watts hymn paraphrasing Psalm 23, "no more a stranger or a guest, but like a child at home."[9] Home in the heart of God's radical hospitality.

Epilogue:
An Easter Epiphany

By late winter in 2003, Washington was shell-shocked. Ceaseless F-16 flyovers, anthrax attacks, sniper shootings, orange-level alerts, duct tape and plastic sheeting, and the possibility of war in Iraq—the city resembled an armed camp. On the morning after the security threat level was raised, the local news reported on the missile batteries deployed around the city. As I watched the television, a bit dazed by the pictures of soldiers guarding Memorial Bridge, I thought to myself: *I live in a city surrounded by missiles*. I figure that one day I will tell my grandchildren that I lived through the siege of Washington. In a sermon on February 2, I borrowed a line from *Richard III* and referred to our contemporary tragedy as the "real 'winter of our discontent.'" The entire congregation nodded in agreement.

Washington's public story, its political one, was, however, quietly intertwined with another tale. As the city feared a potential terrorist attack and waited for impending war, God's people, like those of us at Church of the Epiphany, went on. We did what we always did—living our lives in relation to the Christian story. During the long stressful months, the liturgical year unfolded as it has for two millennia. Terror threats? War? No matter. Pentecost yielded to Advent; Advent opened to Christmas; Christmas gave way to Epiphany; Epiphany led to Lent; and Lent ushered us to Easter. On Sundays, snipers and terrorists seemed less threatening as we walked the way of faith: waiting, birth, revelation, repentance, and resurrection. No matter the anxiety of the City of Man, God's time went on.

Through many of those long months, I wanted to run away. I rued moving to the Washington area, regretted that my daughter lived in such a place. I wished I lived in Dubuque or Flagstaff—somewhere in the "middle," far from the *Washington Post* and its daily recitation of the variety of ways terrorists could kill us and the likelihood of biological attack or radiological warfare. In Washington, September 11 never really ended. It just goes on and on.

I did not, however, run away. I went to church. Church in the city. Month after month, season after season, I journeyed with God through the Christian year; and I heard the familiar story in a new context—against the backdrop of terrorism, violence, and war. I never realized how sad the Christian story could be. How longing and loving. How raw and shocking. How powerful and startling. Halfway through Lent, I was spiritually begging for mercy. I wanted it all to be over. I wanted it all to be true. I longed for Easter.

As it always does, Easter finally arrived. The weather was glorious, warm and sunny after a long, cold, and snowy winter.

Flowers, bushes, and trees bloomed in full spring splendor. My family dressed and hurried to church for worship and the Easter egg hunt. Richard and I were scheduled to read prayers. Emma and Mpho, another five-year-old girl from the Sunday school, had been asked to help with the Easter offering. The church was full of people. The music was just as it should be on Easter morning—joyful and triumphant.

Emma and Mpho looked adorable in their ruffled spring dresses. They carried ribboned baskets for the collection. Parishioners bypassed the traditional plates in order to give their Easter envelopes to the little girls. After the collection, they waited in the back of the church to come down the aisle with the offerings of money, bread, and wine. When the music sounded, the offertory processional started. I was so proud of Emma—how grown-up she looked. From my pew, I strained to see her walk down that aisle as the congregation stood around me.

Through the crowd, I caught sight of her. Emma and Mpho were holding hands and walking toward the table with such joy that their gait could rightly be called skipping. Two little girls, one white and one black, holding hands—practically dancing down the aisle on Easter morning. With trumpets sounding, they embodied all that Epiphany hopes to be.

Watching them, I heard the words of a sermon in my mind. Not the just preached Easter sermon. But a sermon of forty years ago, also preached in Washington, D.C. A sermon preached when I was four years old. I was not present to hear it back in 1963, but I have nearly memorized it. "I have a dream," said the preacher, "that one day little black boys and black girls will be able to join hands with little white boys and white girls and walk together as sisters and brothers."[1]

And there it was: Martin Luther King Jr.'s dream on an Easter morning in frilly pastel dresses prancing down the aisle at Church of the Epiphany. Two little girls, bound in friendship and faith, oblivious to both skin color and their ancestral history of racial violence and hatred. One born in an ancient line of immigrants who settled in Jamestown, Virginia; the other born of recent immigrants from South Africa. Both baptized into the body of Christ, children of the church. Forty years after his sermon, in a congregation in the heart of Washington, D.C., a dream was being realized. An American dream. A Christian dream. A kingdom dream. When I was a little girl, many people thought his dream was wrong, ridiculous, or impossible. "Never happen," my relatives opined.

That is what it means, I thought. To be a faithful alien citizen. To dream that the Christian story can make a difference in the world. To live a story of peace, reconciliation, love, and justice. To believe that there can be a place where people are free from oppression and fear. To give one's life to God's hope for humankind no matter the cost. Suddenly, in the most unlikely way and place, I felt proud to be an American. That Easter Sunday was more of an epiphany than a resurrection. With Emma and Mpho leading the way, I could see something that I had not been able to see very clearly since September 11. I could see love. I could see God's love changing people. Making a difference. Opening the way to a better world. I knew there was hope.

I did not want to flee. I did not feel angry or sad or afraid. I did not want to run away from the tensions and paradox of Christian citizenship. I could say with Martin Luther King Jr., "With this faith we will be able to transform the jangling discords of our nation into a beautiful symphony of brotherhood."[2] Forty years later, however, it must be a global nation, a "beautiful symphony" of common humanity, compassion, and love. Not just black and white. But Christian and Muslim and Jew and atheist and agnostic and Hindu and Buddhist. I thought of St. Paul's description of God's household as revealed through Jesus Christ, "You are no longer Jew nor Greek, male nor female, slave nor free. You are all one" (Gal. 3:28). God is calling us to hold hands across the deepest divides known to humankind, the ways in which we understand divine will and purpose of life. God wants us to be the long-promised household of peace. Theologian Larry Rasmussen writes of this as the "world church": "'World Church' identifies a global people serving as a witness from *among* the nations *to* the nations, in the interests of a world community seeking to live in peace."[3] Emma and Mpho. The *oikos* of *shalom*. The embodiment of world church.

I know it will be incredibly hard. I know we must be incredibly wise. Many people ridicule God's dream. They say it is impossible, idealistic, unrealistic. *Unsafe*. That it plays into the hands of our enemies. But what else does being an alien citizen mean but living the resurrection and an Easter life right in the heart of Washington, D.C.? In these long months, the *oikos* of *shalom* has begun to feel real to me, as if it is waiting on the other side of an invisible door. The door of this national dark night of the soul. The door of the cross.

134

I wanted to skip down the aisle with those little girls, my basket filled with offerings to God. I wondered if they too could feel the reality of the dream.

The Easter anthems sounded loud and clear and true. The girls handed their baskets over the table to the priest. Emma turned to the congregation smiling and ran back to me with open arms.

I opened my arms and embraced her. *Dreams do come true,* I thought as I wiped Easter tears from my eyes, *dreams do come true.* Idealistic ones. Improbable ones. *American dreams. Kingdom dreams.*

Notes

Introduction

1. R. Bellah, *The Broken Covenant* (New York: Seabury Press, 1975), p. 142.
2. W. C. Roof and W. McKinney, *American Mainline Religion* (New Brunswick, N.J.: Rutgers University Press, 1987), p. 34.
3. R. C. White Jr., "Lincoln's Sermon on the Mount: The Second Inaugural," in R. M. Miller, H. S. Stout, and C. R. Wilson (eds.), *Religion and the American Civil War* (New York: Oxford University Press, 1998), p. 209.
4. M. Noll, *One Nation Under God? Christian Faith and Political Action in America* (San Francisco: HarperSanFrancisco, 1988), p. 102.
5. R. Niebuhr, *The Irony of American History* (New York: Scribner, 1952), p. 172.
6. M. Marty, "Two Kinds of Civil Religion," in R. Bellah and D. Jones (eds.), *American Civil Religion* (New York: HarperCollins, 1974), pp. 139–157.
7. R. Jewett and J. S. Lawrence, *Captain America and the Crusade Against Evil* (Grand Rapids, Mich.: Eerdmans, 2003).

Chapter One, Broken We Kneel

1. C. P. McIlvaine, "Bishop's Address," *Journals of the Diocese of Ohio* (Columbus, Ohio: Nevins, 1861), p. 15.

2. B. Harvey, *Another City: An Ecclesiological Primer for a Post-Christian World* (Harrisburg, Pa.: Trinity Press, 1999).
3. Augustine, *The City of God* (New York: Modern Library, 1950), 1:35.
4. T. Merton, "Introduction," in Augustine, *City of God*, p. ix.
5. Augustine, *City of God*, 19:17.
6. Augustine, *City of God*, 19:17.
7. Augustine, *City of God*, 1:8.
8. R. Greer, *Broken Lights and Mended Lives: Theology and Common Life in the Early Church* (University Park: Pennsylvania State University Press, 1986), p. 205.
9. Greer, *Broken Lights*, p. 158.
10. Epistle to Diogentus 5:5, in Loeb Classical Library 25, *The Apostolic Fathers,* Vol. 2, ed. and trans. B. Ehrman (Cambridge, Mass.: Harvard University Press, 2003).
11. Greer, *Broken Lights,* pp. 141–161.
12. M. Noll, "Lutheran Difference," *First Things*, 1992, *2,* p. 37.
13. P. Brown, *Augustine of Hippo* (Berkeley: University of California Press, 1967), p. 325.
14. Augustine, *City of God*, 22:30.
15. Harvey, *Another City,* p. 25.

Chapter Two, "And a Little Child . . ."

1. S. Hauerwas, "Radical Hope," in J. Berkman and M. Cartwright (eds.), *The Hauerwas Reader* (Durham, N.C.: Duke University Press, 2001), p. 517.
2. L. G. Jones, "Forgiveness," in D. C. Bass (ed.), *Practicing Our Faith: A Way of Life for a Searching People* (San Francisco: Jossey-Bass, 1997), p. 134.
3. Jones, "Forgiveness," p. 136.
4. Martin Luther King Jr., *Strength to Love* (New York: HarperCollins, 1963), p. 38.
5. D. Bonhoeffer, *Letters and Papers from Prison,* ed. E. Bethge (London: SCM Press, 1967), p. 172.
6. J. Gundry-Volf, "The Least and the Greatest: Children in the New

Testament," in M. Bunge (ed.), *The Child in Christian Thought* (Grand Rapids, Mich.: Eerdmans, 2001), p. 39.

7. Gundry-Volf, "The Least and the Greatest," p. 37.
8. S. Cavalleti, *The Religious Potential of the Child* (Mt. Ranier, Md.: Catechesis of the Good Shepherd, 1992), pp. 43, 142.

Chapter Three, "God Bless America" and "Amazing Grace"

1. M. Rourke and E. Gwathmey, *Amazing Grace in America: Our Spiritual National Anthem* (Santa Monica, Calif.: Angel City, 1996).
2. L. Bergreen, *As Thousands Cheer: The Life of Irving Berlin* (New York: Penguin, 1991), p. 382.
3. W. Herberg, *Protestant-Catholic-Jew: An Essay in American Religious Sociology* (New York: Doubleday, 1955).
4. R. Wuthnow, *After Heaven: Spirituality in America Since the 1950s* (Berkeley: University of California Press, 1998).
5. Jewett and Lawrence, *Captain America,* p. 8.
6. R. S. Bridges, after J. Neader (c. 1680), "All My Hope on God Is Founded," from *The Hymnal, 1982* (New York: Church Hymnal Corp., 1985), no. 665.
7. J. Winthrop, "A Model of Christian Charity," quoted in R. Mathisen, *The Role of Religion in American Life: An Interpretive Historical Anthology* (Lanham, Md.: University Press of America, 1982), pp. 9–19.

Chapter Four, Going to the Chapel

1. A. Schmemann, *For the Life of the World: Sacraments and Orthodoxy* (Crestwood, N.Y.: St. Vladimirs, 1973).
2. S. Hauerwas and W. Willimon, *Resident Aliens: Life in the Christian Colony* (Nashville, Tenn.: Abingdon Press, 1989).
3. R. Finke and R. Stark, *The Churching of America, 1776–1990: Winners and Losers in Our Religious Economy* (New Brunswick, N.J.: Rutgers University Press, 1992).
4. World Council of Churches, *Baptism, Eucharist, and Ministry* (Geneva, Switzerland: World Council of Churches, 1982), p. 20.

5. G. Marsden, *Religion and American Culture* (Orlando, Fla.: Harcourt, 1990), p. 116.

6. Marsden, *Religion and American Culture,* p. 116.

7. Hauerwas and Willimon, *Resident Aliens,* p. 66.

8. Jan W., "St. Paul's Chapel Message Board" [http://www. saintpaulschapel.org], Mar. 14, 2002, accessed April 2003.

9. F. Burnham, "It Was What I Call a Foretaste of the Kingdom," [http://www.trinitywallstreet.org/news/alert_194.shtml], n.d., accessed April 2003.

10. V. Havner, quoted in M. H. Manser (comp.), *Westminster Collection of Christian Quotations* (Louisville, Ky.: Westminster/John Knox, 2001), p. 44.

11. E. Kennedy, *9-11: Meditation at the Center of the World* (Maryknoll, N.Y.: Orbis, 2002), p. 98.

Chapter Five, Compassionate Imperialism?

1. M. Ignatieff, "The American Empire: The Burden," *New York Times Magazine,* Jan. 5, 2003, p. 22.

2. M. Ignatieff, "Nation Building Lite," *New York Times Magazine,* July 28, 2002, pp. 26ff.

3. R. Horsley, *Jesus and Empire: The Kingdom of God and the New World Disorder* (Minneapolis, Minn.: Fortress, 2003), pp. 14, 126.

4. Horsley, *Jesus and Empire,* p. 133.

5. Harvey, *Another City,* p. 57.

6. B. Winter, "Roman Law and Society in Romans 12–15," in P. Oakes (ed.), *Rome in the Bible and the Early Church* (Grand Rapids, Mich.: Baker, 2002), p. 75.

7. Horsley, *Jesus and Empire,* p. 134.

8. Greer, *Broken Lights,* p. 103.

9. D. Chidester, *Christianity: A Global History* (San Francisco: HarperSanFrancisco, 2000), p. 94.

10. "Bush and God," *Newsweek,* Mar. 10, 2003, p. 24.

11. R. H. Bainton, *The Church of Our Fathers* (New York: Scribner, 1941), pp. 38–39.

12. Chidester, *Christianity,* pp. 91–92.

13. V. Dozier, *The Dream of God: A Call to Return* (Cambridge, Mass.: Cowley, 1991), p. 72.

14. B. Bailyn, *The Ideological Origins of the American Revolution* (Cambridge, Mass.: Harvard University Press, 1967), p. 25.

15. R. H. Seager, *The World's Parliament of Religions: The East-West Encounter, Chicago, 1893* (Bloomington: Indiana University Press, 1995), pp. 3–4.

16. G. W. Bush, "Address," in *God Is Our Comfort and Strength: National Day of Prayer and Remembrance Service, September 14, 2001* (Washington, D.C.: Washington National Cathedral, 2001), p. 9.

17. W. Berry, "A Citizen's Response to the National Security Strategy of the United States of America," *New York Times,* Feb. 9, 2003 [paid advertisement].

18. S. Hauerwas, "How 'Christian Ethics' Came to Be," in Berkman and Cartwright, *Hauerwas Reader,* p. 39.

19. Horsley, *Jesus,* p. 5.

20. Hauerwas, "How 'Christian Ethics' Came to Be," p. 39.

Chapter Six, Homeland Security

1. F.B.P., "Jerusalem, My Happy Home," in *The Hymnal, 1982* (New York: Church Hymnal Corp., 1985), no. 620.

2. M. Cromartie (ed.), *No Longer Exiles: The New Religious Right in American Politics* (Washington, D.C.: Ethics and Public Policy Center, 1993).

3. A. Wolfe, *The Transformation of American Religion: How We Actually Live Our Faith* (New York: Free Press, 2003), p. 4.

4. Harvey, *Another City,* p. 33.

5. M. Lienesch, *Redeeming America: Piety and Politics in the New Christian Right* (Chapel Hill: University of North Carolina, 1993).

6. Hauerwas and Willimon, *Resident Aliens,* p. 49.

7. Harvey, *Another City,* p. 162.

8. H. Thurman, "The Task of the Negro Ministry," in W. E. Flunker and C. Tumber (eds.), *A Strange Freedom: The Best of Howard Thurman*

on Religious Experience and Public Life (Boston: Beacon Press, 1998), p. 194.

9. D. Soelle, *The Window of Vulnerability: A Political Spirituality* (Minneapolis, Minn.: Fortress, 1990), pp. ix–x.

10. Soelle, *Window of Vulnerability*, p. 4.

11. I. Watts, "O God Our Help in Ages Past," in *The Hymnal, 1982* (New York: Church Hymnal Corp., 1985), p. 680.

12. W. Brueggemann, *Peace* (St. Louis, Mo.: Chalice, 2001), p. 20.

13. Brueggemann, *Peace*, pp. 13–14.

14. Brueggemann, *Peace*, p. 14.

15. Brueggemann, *Peace*, p. 15.

Chapter Seven, Peace and the City

1. G. Keillor, "Episcopal," in D. Armentrout and R. Slocum (eds.), *Documents of Witness: A History of the Episcopal Church, 1782–1985* (New York: Church Hymnal Corp., 1994), p. 624.

2. Soelle, *Window of Vulnerability*.

3. C. Pohl, *Making Room: Recovering Hospitality as a Christian Tradition* (Grand Rapids, Mich.: Eerdmans, 1999), p. x.

4. Pohl, *Making Room*, pp. 61, 62.

5. Pohl, *Making Room*, p. 105; emphasis mine.

6. Pohl, *Making Room*, pp. 105, 124.

7. A. House, *Francis of Assisi* (Mahwah, N.J.: Hidden Spring, 2001), p. 202.

8. House, *Francis of Assisi*, pp. 217–218.

9. I. Watts, "My Shepherd Will Supply My Need," in *The Hymnal, 1982* (New York: Church Hymnal Corp., 1985), no. 664.

Epilogue

1. M. L. King Jr., "I Have a Dream," quoted in E. S. Gaustad (ed.), *A Documentary History of Religion in American Since 1865* (Grand Rapids, Mich.: Eerdmans, 1983), p. 497.

2. King, "I Have a Dream," p. 497.

3. L. Rasmussen, "The Congregation: Moral Convener in a World House?" *Congregations*, Fall 2003, p. 20.

The Author

Diana Butler Bass, born in Baltimore, Maryland, in 1959, was baptized in a Methodist church in her hometown when she was three months old. Her mother, a campaign worker in the 1960 presidential elections, claims that her daughter's first words were "Dada," "Mama," and "John Kennedy." Thus began a lifelong interest in both religion and politics.

Bass holds a Ph.D. in American religious history from Duke University and is the author of two critically acclaimed books. The more recent, *Strength for the Journey: A Pilgrimage of Faith in Community* (Jossey-Bass, 2002), earned a starred review in *Publishers Weekly,* which named it one of the best religion books of 2002. Her dissertation, published as *Standing Against the Whirlwind: Evangelical Episcopalians in Nineteenth-Century America* (Oxford University Press, 1995), won the Frank S. and Elizabeth D. Brewer prize of the American Society of Church History. She has taught at Westmont College, the University of California at Santa Barbara, Macalester College, and Rhodes

College. In addition to her scholarly work, from 1995 to 2000 she wrote a weekly column on American religion for the New York Times Syndicate.

Currently, she is senior research fellow and director of the Project on Congregations of Intentional Practice, a Lilly Endowment–funded study of mainline Protestant vitality—a project featured on Beliefnet.com and in the *Los Angeles Times*—at the Virginia Theological Seminary in Alexandria, Virginia. She teaches religion and politics, church history, and congregational studies. She is currently working on three books: *Going to Church: Religion and Spirituality in Contemporary American Protestantism, Practicing Congregations: Emerging Mainline Churches,* and *Episcopalians in America.*

She lives with her husband, Richard Bass, and their six-year-old daughter, Emma, in Alexandria, Virginia, where they are joined during part of the year by her teenage stepson, Jonah. She is a member of the Church of the Epiphany in downtown Washington, D.C. In addition to her family and church, she loves mystery novels, the National Gallery and the Smithsonian, wine tasting, walking, Duke basketball, and the Outer Banks in North Carolina.

Other Books of Interest

Strength for the Journey:
A Pilgrimage of Faith in Community
Diana Butler Bass
Hardcover
ISBN: 0–7879–5578–7

"Embroidering her commentary with the intricate knots and binding strands of the Church's history among us, Bass renders for us a new fabric of many colors and invites us to shelter ourselves within its triumphant folds. She also, as I have said from the very beginning, thereby creates something of a post-modern amazement."

—From the Foreword by Phyllis Tickle

"Diana Butler Bass has written a rare kind of book. Part religious travelogue, part contemporary tracing of one pilgrim's progress, part spiritual autobiography, *Strength for the Journey* gives us a very personal and a very acute view of what life is like for a committed Christian today."

—James P. Wind, president, The Alban Institute

"A compelling intertwining of a personal spiritual journey and the recent history of Protestantism. Diana Butler Bass makes the case that baby boom seekers are drawing the Church into a new, more authentic Christianity."

—Nora Gallagher, author,
Things Seen and Unseen: A Year Lived in Faith

In *Strength for the Journey,* Diana Butler Bass illustrates the dynamic strength and persistence of mainline Protestantism. While many baby boomers left the church, only to come back later in life, Bass was a "stayer" who witnessed the struggles and changes and found much there that was meaningful. Offering thought-provoking portraits of eight parishes she attended over two decades, she explores the major issues that have confronted mainline denominations, congregations, and parishioners during those years—from debates over women clergy to conflicts about diversity and community to scrimmages between tradition and innovation.

Diana Butler Bass's story reveals the church's history among us. She uses her life as the focal point to tell the larger story of contemporary mainline church life, with all of its ups and downs. During the last two decades, she says, "the church was being quietly transformed by the experiences of stayers like myself who demanded different visions and practices of churchgoing than the institution had traditionally offered." And out of the turbulence, a new kind of mainline congregation has been emerging, and a new period of American Protestantism is being born.